Education in
Washington, DC

Education in Washington, DC

Edited by
Abdul Karim Bangura

iUniverse, Inc.
New York Lincoln Shanghai

Education in Washington, DC

iUniverse books may be ordered through booksellers or by contacting:

iUniverse
2021 Pine Lake Road, Suite 100
Lincoln, NE 68512
www.iuniverse.com
1-800-Authors (1-800-288-4677)

ISBN: 978-0-595-48033-3 (pbk)
ISBN: 978-0-595-60133-2 (ebk)

Printed in the United States of America

Washington, DC Youth

Contents

Acknowledgments

We, and hopefully many readers, owe gratitude to:

Professors Alvin Thornton, Lorenzo Morris, Maurice Woodard and Michael Frazier, for encouraging this type of scholarship.

Professor Charles Harris, for his quiet and gentle inspiration.

Ms. Javenia Lily, Mrs. Saphronia Drake, and Ms. Brentina Taylor, for their genuine friendship and administrative assistance.

Yiesha Thompson, for effulgent research and keyboarding assistance.

The numerous families to which we belong, for offering their encouragement and prayers.

1

General Introduction

✦

Abdul Karim Bangura

This is our fifth in a series of books dealing with Washington, DC (District of Columbia). The first book, *Historical Political Economy of Washington, DC*, was published by University Press of America in 2000. The second, third and fourth books, *DC Vote: Fighting Against Taxation Without Representation, Washington, DC State of Affairs*, and *Washington, DC's Challenges*, were published by Writers Press in 2001, 2003, and 2005, respectively. All of these books are outgrowths of special seminars conducted in the Department of Political Science at Howard University.

The present book is also a result of two seminars conducted at Howard University in the fall of 2005 and the spring of 2006. The chapters in this book are revised versions of selected papers that were presented at the seminars. The major focus of the chapters is on the educational challenges and triumphs in Washington, DC. We examine education in Washington, DC because it is vital to know the conditions under which the residents of the most powerful city in the world are being trained in the academic arena, based on sound empirical evidence.

During his campaign for the Washington, DC Office of Mayor, Democratic Party candidate Adrian Fenty made education his central theme, because he believes that it is the most important factor that is keeping the District from achieving all that it could. Is Fenty correct? You bet! As this book demonstrates, the empirical evidence and the residents of DC seem to agree.

Education in Washington, DC, as the following chapters reveal, is a mixed phenomenon. On the one hand, Washington, DC's public schools are among the lowest performing schools in the nation; on the other hand, four of the city's universities (Catholic, Georgetown, George Washington, and Howard) are ranked among the 500 best universities (out of thousands) in the world according to the most scientific and comprehensive survey on raking schools conducted by a group of Chinese social scientists (http://ed.sjtu.edu.cn/ranking.htm). Instead of rehashing the state of Washington, DC's education, which is thoroughly done in the ensuing chapters, what I do in the rest of this chapter is discuss how the District can transform its failing public schools and the work of the many organizations that advocate education policy in the city.

Transforming the Public Schools

The following lessons for transforming educational systems provided the Basic Education Coalition (1994) are quite germane for DC's public education. While no single education model exists and education must be flexible to fit local, national and international dynamics and differing levels of development, the following elements are common to many successful education systems:

a. Students must be healthy and nourished, and their learning must be supported at home.

b. Teachers must have proper and continuous training and administrative support, and they must encourage active learning and participation by students.

c. Curricula and materials relevant to local, national and international needs and contexts must be developed and used.

d. Parent and community engagement is imperative so that teachers are comfortable sending their daughters and sons to school.

e.   Flexible instruction, including alternative delivery formats, classroom hours, and content are needed, in order to meet the particular needs of out-of-school children and their families.

f.   Transparent school management and an administration with adequate training that is accountable to stakeholders and constituents and capable of monitoring and evaluating school performance are imperative.

g.   Funding that ensures education infrastructure, materials and personnel are a must.

Education determines the prospects of people and countries. Evidence is compelling that, while not sufficient by itself, education is a prerequisite for economic development, individual health and well-being, democracy, and poverty alleviation. Basic education, which encompasses early childhood development through early secondary schools, is considered an antidote to the spread of both HIV/AIDS and child abuse. Studies link education to higher economic productivity, longer life expectancy rates, lower infant mortality rates, and greater tolerance. Education empowers people and gives them a stake in society.

Over the last decade, increased attention to the plight of children out of school and a greater understanding of the toll that large uneducated populations impose on a country have spurred advances in education. Worldwide, adult illiteracy rates fell from 25 percent in 1990 to 21 percent in 2000. During the 1990s, primary-school enrollments increased in all regions of the world.

Education alone is not sufficient to generate development. But undeniably, no substantial gains will derive from other investments without suitable education investments and progress. No country has reached sustained economic growth without attaining near universal basic education. Economic research has found that one year of additional education increases individual output by 4-7 percent, and countries that improve literacy rates by 20-30 percent have seen increases in gross domestic product (GDP) of 8-16 percent. Heavy investment in primary education and tight management of the investment are the most important factors in the difference between economic boom and slow growth.

Education equips individuals with the knowledge and skills to lead healthier lives and creates a cycle of improved opportunities for children. Educated people live longer. Multi-country research has shown that the education of children—particularly girls—is correlated with lower death rates. According to in-country longitudinal estimates, a 10-percent increase in primary enrollment rates is associated with an average 10.8-month increase in life expectancy.

Mothers with basic education have healthier pregnancies. They are more likely to seek pre-and post-natal care and follow doctors' recommendations. They are more proactive about illness, negotiate better healthcare for themselves and their families, and are more aware of preventive measures such as vaccinations. Indeed, as secondary school enrollment rates for girls increase, rates of immunization for children less than 12 months of age also increase. Educated mothers also provide better hygiene and nutrition for their children. According to data from 35 recent demographic and health surveys, children of mothers with no education are more than twice as likely to die or to be malnourished than children of mothers who have secondary education or higher, even when controlling for other factors. In fact, the education level of a mother is a better predictor of child health than even the general socioeconomic status of the family. A study of 53 countries found that an increase in women's education levels was the most significant determinant in the 15.5 percent drop in child malnutrition between 1970 and 1995.

Educated women have greater control over their own reproductive lives. Women with secondary education tend to have significantly fewer children than uneducated women; they marry later and space their pregnancies better, reducing health risks to both themselves and their children. As girls' enrollment rates increase and child survival rates improve, family size decreases. Education plays a pivotal role in falling fertility rates, because it empowers women with greater decision-making abilities so that fertility preferences can be implemented effectively.

For girls, children with disabilities, and youth vulnerable to HIV/AIDS, basic education provides the knowledge and life skills necessary to make informed choices, and helps individuals cope with difficult life circumstances. Better-educated girls tend to postpone sex and are more likely to require their partners to use condoms. World Bank research on 32 countries found that women with post-primary education were three times more likely than uneducated women to know that HIV can be transmitted from mother to child.

Education is highly cost effective; it brings together students, teachers, parents, and the community, all of whom play a vital role in preventing HIV/AIDS. It reduces vulnerability to the disease by providing children with practical skills, additional access to adults they can trust, improved sense of security and connectedness, and increased literacy. Simply keeping children in school longer is a defense against HIV/AIDS. Since HIV/AIDS is a preventable disease with no known cure, basic education remains the strongest weapon against it.

Often, it makes a crucial difference in children's lives by giving them the knowledge to deal with health issues and the skills to achieve a better future. Education helps to empower girls and diminish gender biases, as well as improve the opportunities of those with disabilities. Schools are a refuge and offer a degree of normalcy in an otherwise chaotic world.

Education also dramatically protects against child abuse and sexual exploitation. Children who attend school are less vulnerable to sexual and other exploitations. A child who does not attend school is a child who, inevitably, will be put to work.

Investments in education generate continuous returns. Children of educated mothers are more likely to succeed in school. These children, in turn, are more likely to encourage their children to attend school, creating a virtuous cycle benefiting future generations and facilitating a broad-based and more equitable national development.

Education is a prerequisite for economic growth. While correlations between measures of education and economic growth are open to interpretation, and scholars debate how to isolate the causal impacts of education on economic development, significant evidence links investments in education to economic growth. A recent synthesis of empirical evidence concluded that economies with larger investments in human capital through education experience faster growth. Additional research has found that education expenditures generate definitive results: 11 out of 12 countries examined in the study show significant, positive effects of educational expenditures on economic growth.

Education provides the knowledge and judgment skills that promote tolerance and understanding among peoples. It also reduces both poverty and inequality, and lays the foundation for sound governance and effective institutions. Studies by the World Bank and Freedom House have found that countries with higher levels of education have stronger democratic rights. As high school enrollment rates rise, rates of political participation also increase. Improving access to primary and secondary education contributes to political participation in part due to per capita economic growth and citizens' enhanced stake in society.

Universal basic education lays the foundation for strengthening democracy. Improved access to and quality of education reduces poverty and inequality and expands the middle and working classes, a key determinant of democratization. Educated people better understand their individual rights and are better equipped to participate politically. Citizens with education are more likely to vote and express more tolerant attitudes and democratic ideals.

Employing student-centered teaching methods, teachers engage students as active participants in the learning process and impart skills that allow them to think critically and act for themselves. Through education, the values and fabric of nations are constructed, making it crucial that instruction promotes broad-based learning and respect for alternative traditions and opinions.

While there is much to be done to ensure that all children have access to quality education, the situation is by no means hopeless. Education for all can be achieved. Time-tested and effective strategies to improve educational access and quality are well known, and the know-how to implement them exists throughout the public, private, and non-governmental sectors. The key to successfully meeting the education challenge is political will—financial and otherwise. While complex and challenging, the solution is within reach.

In essence, quality education is not a luxury to be addressed once the DC government gets the rest of its house in order. Evidence shows that it is a precursor for all factors of development: economic growth, poverty reduction, health, and environmental sustainability. It is linked to better governance and stability. Quality education will nurture the human capacity of Washington, DC's residents, across generations.

Organizations Advocating Education Policy

The following are brief descriptions of the organizations with offices in Washington, DC that advocate education policy. While all of them share a vision for quality education in the District and beyond, they do differ in terms of their foci and operations (visit http://education-policy.com/DC.html).

Academy for Economic Development

Founded in 1961, the Academy for Economic development (AED) is an independent, nonprofit service organization committed to addressing human development needs in the United States and around the world. Under contracts and grants, AED operates programs in collaboration with policy makers, non-governmental organizations (NGOs), businesses, government agencies, schools, colleges and universities. The organization works on issues including, but not limited to, adult learning, education reform, school to work, and youth development (http://www.aed.org).

American Association of Higher Education

The American Association of Higher Education (AAHE) envisions a higher education enterprise that helps all Americans achieve the deep, life-long learning they need to grow as individuals, participate in the democratic process, and succeed in the global economy. The AAHE is a membership organization that strongly advocates the changes that higher education must make for greater effectiveness. It collaborates with other organizations with similar goals. By sharing information via conferences, publications, projects, partnerships, special interest groups and network-ing, the AAHE seeks to make a positive difference in the field of education (http://www.aahe.org).

American Council on Education

Founded in 1918, the American Council on Education (ACE) is the venue where all American higher education converges. The ACE works to advance access and quality in American higher education. The organiza-tion deals with a full spectrum of public policy issues affecting American colleges and universities, including issues of quality and accreditation, diversity, financial aid resources, research funding, tax policy, technology and college costs. It serves as a powerful advocate on Capitol Hill and beyond when it deals with these and other national issues of importance to campuses nationwide (http://acenet.edu).

American Federation of Teachers

The American Federation of Teachers (AFT) is a union built on demo-cratic values and is devoted to those it serves as much as to its members. The AFT fights for the preservation and improvement of public educa-tion. Past members of the AFT included some great contributors to educa-tion such as John Dewey and Albert Einstein. The AFT is one of the fastest growing unions in the United States. Some of the organization's major education initiatives include "Lessons for Life: Responsibility, Respect, Results," which represent a national campaign to achieve higher academic and disciplinary standards; and "Making Standards Matter," which is an annual report on efforts to raise academic standards in each of the 50 states and the District of Columbia. Also, the AFT has helped to get "Zero Tolerance" laws passed in many states and DC to ensure that students learn in safe school settings (http://www.aft.org).

American Institute for Research

Founded in 1946, the American Institute for Research (AIR) is an inde-pendent, nonprofit corporation that performs basic and applied research and evaluations, provides technical support, and conducts quantitative and qualitative analyses in the behavioral and social sciences. The organization's research areas include education reform and assessment, education finance, international and comparative education, special education, and education statistics (http://www.air-dc.org).

Belden Russonello and Stewart—Research and Communications

A research and communications firm, Belden Russonello and Stewart helps clients to better understand their public. The organization provides research-based strategic advise and planning to educational organizations, nonprofit organizations, political campaigns, and others. It specializes in employing survey research, polls, focus groups and research analysis to present a high quality product to its clients (http://www.brs@brspoll.com).

Center for Education Reform

Founded in 1993, the Center for Education Reform (CER) is an independent, nonprofit advocacy organization that provides support to individuals working to bring fundamental reforms to their schools. The organization works with parents, teachers, school administrators, business and community leaders, and local and state legislators to connect policy and practice in order to advance ideas that are critical to the future of the quality of education in the United States. The CER acts as a clearinghouse of information on innovative education reforms and works hand-in-hand with states and communities across America on issues such as school choice, charter schools, and standards (http://www,edreform.com).

Center for Equal Opportunity

The Center for Equal Opportunity (CEO) is a private, nonprofit research institution founded in 1995. The Center challenges the policies that divide the United States and segregate its ethnic groups. It is dedicated to the notion that America should be one united nation and its citizens of all colors should be treated with equal protection under the laws, as the Constitution stipulates. The organization concentrates on the following areas:

racial preferences, immigration and assimilation, and multicultural education (http://www.ceousa.org).

Character Education Partnership

The Character Education Partnership (CEP) is a nonpartisan coalition of organizations and individuals who are concerned about the moral crisis confronting America's youth. The CEP is dedicated to developing moral character in young people as one way to promote a more compassionate and responsible society. The organization believes that character education helps students to identify and act with universally accepted values like honesty, fairness, responsibility and respect (http://www.character.org).

Council for Basic Education

For more than 40 years, the Council for Basic Education (CBE) has promoted a curriculum that focuses strongly on the teaching and learning of the basic subjects for all students including English and foreign languages, history, government, mathematics, geography, the sciences, and the arts. The CBE is an independent voice calling for educational excellence. It is a nonprofit organization that focuses on these issues in order to develop the capacity for lifelong learning and the creation of responsible citizens. The organization seeks to meet these objectives through publishing periodicals and administering practical programs to teachers, schools, business leaders, concerned citizens and policymakers (http://www.c-b-e.org).

Council of Chief State School Officers

The Council of Chief State School Officers (CCSSO) is a nonprofit organization composed of public officials who head the departments of elementary and secondary education. The CCSSO has served as an independent voice on federal education policy since 1927. The organization assists states with new policy initiatives, and it assists the federal government in implementing new programs. It widely distributes research studies and reports on education policy to interested parties nationwide (http://ccsso.org).

Council of Great City Schools

The Council of Great City Schools (CGCS) is an organization made up of the largest urban public school systems. The CGCS advocates better K-12 education in inner city schools. It is governed by superintendents and board of education members from 50 cities across the United States (http://www.chcs.org).

Education Policy Institute

Founded in 1995, the Education Policy Institute (EPI) is a nonprofit education organization that seeks to provide an alternative, market-oriented voice to the education reform movement. The EPI works to improve education through research, policy analysis, and the development of responsible alternatives to existing policies and practices. The organization strives to promote greater parental choice in education, a more competitive education industry, a more creative role for the for-profit sector, and other policies that address problems of both public and private schools (http://www.educationpolicy.org).

Educause

Educase seeks to help shape and enable transformational change in higher education through the introduction, use and management of information resources and technologies in teaching, learning, scholarship, research and institutional management. Educause advocates higher education policy issues, tries to influence policy makers who have a stake in transformational information technologies, and acts as a catalyst for policy issues and a conduit for communication among professionals with common interests and concerns (http://www.educause.edu).

Empower America

Empower America (EA) says it is the most dynamic policy organization in the United States. EA is an advocacy organization that seeks to steer public policy in favor of individual freedom and opportunity, responsibility and excellence. The organization practices strategic interventions to achieve its goals, which include education reform and choice (http://www.empower.org).

Future Quest, Inc.

Future Quest is an educational consulting firm that specializes in educational planning and college placement. It offers college counseling, Standardized Aptitude Test (SAT) preparation courses, and one-on-one sessions with students and families (http://www.futurequest.org).

Institute for Educational Leadership Policy Exchange

The Institute for Educational Leadership Policy Exchange (IELPE) focuses on public policies affecting children and families. The IELPE works with Congress, the administration and agencies that write and administer programs for children and families. It emphasizes accountability and results by defining and measuring what is in the forefront of education policy. The IELPE is a nonpartisan organization that seeks to improve educational opportunities and results for children, youth and families by bridging the gap between developing and supporting leaders in the field of education. The organization distributes publications dealing with frontline education issues and emerging trends (http://www.policyexchange.iel.org).

National Alliance of Business

The National Alliance of Business (NAB) is a national, nonprofit, business-led organization that focuses solely on human resources issues. It commits the bulk of its time and resources to substantive policy and project work. It represents the business point of view on policy issues that affect the nation's workforce. It believes that the key to maximizing corporate productivity and worker security is by focusing on both training and education. The NAB pays particular attention to policy issues ranging from worker training to K-12 education reform (http://www.nab.com).

National Association of Independent Schools

A voluntary membership organization, the National Association of Independent Schools (NAIS) advocates for independent pre-collegiate education nationwide. The NAIS tracks and analyzes legislation and regulation on environmental health hazards, tax, and education. The organization keeps the education community informed about these issues. There exist approximately 111,500 schools in the United States; of this number, 1,004 are independent schools that are members of the NAIS. Independent schools are primarily supported by tuitions, charitable contributions and endowment rather than by tax or church funds. Many NAIS member schools offer school based teacher preparatory programs for inexperienced or prospective teachers (http://www.nais-schools.org).

National Center on Education and the Economy

The National Center for Education and the Economy (NCEE) is a non-profit organization that focuses on standards-based reform. It believes that education and training systems works best when clear standards are set for student achievement, the standards are measured and integrated, and people are then held accountable for student progress. The organization promotes the idea that students must take responsibility for their own learning. It helps states and localities build the capacity to design and implement their own education and training systems suited to their own unique needs (http://www.ncee.org).

National Education Association

The largest and most influential teachers union in the United States, the National Education Association (NEA) has over two million members who work at every level of education. The organization focuses on making education better in as many ways as is possible. Education policy is only one of the NEA's areas of expertise (http://www.nea.org).

National Governors Association

The National Governors Association (NGA) has an education policy division that focuses on all State Governors' policies dealing with education. The organization monitors salient topics in each state and reports on all education policy laws that affect each state (http://www.nga.org).

New Standards Project

The New Standards Project (NSP) provides information to the public on all new performance standards, which are based on the national content standards developed by professional organizations. The performance standards comprise what students should know and ways they should demonstrate their knowledge and skills in each subject (http://www.lrdc.pitt.edu/Institute/NSHomepage.html).

Policy Studies Associates, Inc.

The Policy Studies Associates (PSA), Inc. is a for profit firm of about 30 researchers and a small support staff who conduct research, evaluations, policy analyses, and other projects in education, training and human related services. The organization was founded in 1982 and specializes in two areas: (1) examination of educational services for special needs populations including, but not limited to, homeless youth and disadvantaged youth who are at risk of dropping out of school; and (2) review of policies and strategies geared toward stimulating education improvement and reform (http://www.psa.org).

Public Education Network

The Public Education Network (PEN) seeks to create systems of public education that result in high achievement for every student. The organization provides training, technical assistance, and information to increase the effectiveness of local education funds as catalysts for systematic reform. Through local education funds, the organization is dedicated to building local communities' capacity to create and sustain long-term changes in their schools and to hold schools accountable for quality public education (http://www.publiceducation.org).

The Brookings Institution

The Brookings Institution is an independent, nonpartisan research organization that seeks to improve the performance of American institutions, the effectiveness of government programs, and the quality of United States public policies. It addresses current and emerging policy challenges and offers practical solutions for addressing them. The Brookings Institution excels in education public policy through leadership development (http://www.brookings.edu).

The Cato Institute

Founded in 1977, the Cato Institute (CI) is a nonpartisan public policy research foundation. The CI seeks to broaden the parameters of public policy debate to allow consideration of more options that are consistent with the principles of limited government, individual liberty and peace. The CI accepts to government funding. The organization has an education policy studies department. It also conducts research and writes about education reform, technology, for-profit schooling, state regulation of private schools and more (http://www.cato.org).

The Heritage Foundation

Founded in 1973, this research and educational organization formulates and promotes conservative public policies based on the principles of free enterprise, limited government, freedom, and traditional American values. The Heritage Foundation conducts research on key policy issues and markets the findings to primary audiences such as members of Congress, policymakers, the news media and the academic and policy communities. The organization produces publications, lectures and more. It is a nonpartisan institution that is funded solely by private financial support (http://www.heritage.org).

The McKenzie Group, Inc.—Educational Consultants

The McKenzie Group (TMG) has for over a decade been on the forefront of the quest to bring the power of knowledge to young people by designing and implementing practical and innovative solutions. The organization's areas of specialty include systematic reform, evaluations, survey research, data collection and analyses, assessments, equality studies, educational audits, state-level reviews, and program implementation. The organization is a minority-owned, woman-owned company and an equal opportunity employer (http://www.mckenziegroup.com).

The National Center for Public Policy Research

The National Center for Public Policy Research (NCPPR) is a communications and research foundation which aims to provide free market solutions for today's public policy problems. The organization is quick in responding to emerging issues including those in the are of education (http://www.nationalcenter.org).

The Urban Institute

Founded in 1968, the Urban Institute (UI) is a nonprofit policy research organization that seeks to sharpen thinking about society's problems and effort to solve them, improve government decisions and their implementation, and increase citizens' awareness about important public choices. The UI prides itself in rigorous analyses, innovative methodology, fresh thinking and technical expertise. Much of the organization's research is multi-disciplinary and blends both qualitative and qualitative approaches to problem solving. The organization has a special education policy division that concentrates on front-line education issues (http://www.urban.org).

Organization of the Rest of the Book

The rest of this book is divided into nine chapters. The first six chapters employ survey research techniques, and the last three chapters use multivariate methods. The chapters cover various institutions at two levels of the American political system—i.e. local and national. Chapter 2 by Ronald C. Clark Jr. is about charter schools; chapter 3 by Autumn Saxton-Ross deals with public schools; chapter 4 by Vernese Edghill examines colleges and universities; chapter 5 by Maryam Labeebah Muhammad looks at the National Education Association; chapter 6 by Yiesha Thompson discusses the United States Congress; chapter 7 by Stan Warren is about the White House; chapter 7 by Vernese Edghill, her second contribution to this volume, deals with private school education; chapter 8 by Ronald

C. Clark Jr., also his second contribution to this book, examines the state of public schools; and chapter 9 by Autumn Saxton-Ross, also her second contribution to this work, looks at the No Child Left Behind Act.

Consequently, the topics examined in this book comprise a close set within which it is easier to see how and why new insights emerged. Occasionally, they show new ideas and rediscoveries.

2

Charter Schools

✦

Ronald C. Clark Jr.

Introduction

Since the enactment of No Child Left Behind (NCLB), student academic achievement in the District has become a preeminent concern for elected officials, bureaucrats, educators, parents, and stakeholders alike. Specifically, the impact of the academic and accountability benchmarks contained in NCLB assisted in exposing the overall ineffectiveness, negligence, and dysfunction of the DC Board of Education (DCBE), Office of District of Columbia Public Schools (DCPS), superintendents and DCPS administrators that possessed significant decision-making responsibility. More importantly, this legislation unmasked and addressed the problematic issues of uncertified teachers, decaying facilities, delays and inability to procure necessary educational resources, technological errors and fiscal recklessness. As such, the DCPS 2005 Strategic Plan, *Declaration of Education,* acknowledged that lapses in each of these areas independently and collectively contributed to the substandard academic performance by the District's children. As a remedy to this faulty leadership and mismanagement inside DCPS, two viable alternatives egressed since the presidential election of 2000 in an effort to reform education in the nation's capital. The first is the re-emergent proposal for increasing the quantity of the District's public charter schools, and the second is the nation's first federally-funded school voucher program that is presently managed by the Washington Scholarship Fund (WSF). Of these two recourses, popularity and

19

support for public charter schools is the most widely accepted and plausible preference by many education reform advocates, District officeholders, and the electorate based on the linear flow of public funding to public charter schools. Yet, notwithstanding this acknowledgement, little is known regarding the governance, operation, performance and contention surrounding the District's public charter schools.

The District of Columbia School Reform Act of 1995 (amended in 1996) placed the District at the forefront of a nationwide experiment in the public charter school movement. This legislation effectively authorized two separate and independent entities: (1) the DCBE (through its Office of Charter Schools) and (2) the DC Public Charter School Board (PCSB) with approval and oversight powers of public charter schools (Schneider, Buckley and Kucsova 2003). Thus, in sharp contrast to the governance and operation of traditional public schools, charter schools report to their own boards of trustees that are largely composed of District residents, parents of children that attend charter schools, and members of the community (Moquete 2002). Likewise, charter schools can be established by any person, group, organization, or post-secondary institution, public, private, or quasi-private (Center for Education Reform 2005). In exchange for legal autonomy and greater academic accountability than traditional public schools, charter schools, endorsed and monitored by the two separate school boards, are uniquely focused; they develop their own curricula, institute innovative teaching methodologies, limit enrollment to District children, and control their environment to meet student needs (Board Facts 2005).

In comparison to the District's traditional public schools, charter institutions are expected to receive the same dollar amount of public funding based on the Uniform Per-Pupil Funding Formula that guarantees equitable treatment of all District public school students (Cane 2001). Unlike their conventional counterparts, however, charter schools control 100% of their annual budgets. Some District public charter schools are specialized according to subject area such as the Arts and Technology Academy Public Charter School and Howard University's Public Charter Middle School for Mathematics and Science. Accordingly, contrary to the mandatory teacher certification standards required by NCLB for traditional public schools, educators in charter schools are not mandated to be certified by any governing body. District public charter schools that fail to meet outlined performance measures, academic accountability standards, and other significant requirements as stipulated in the agreement between the DCBE, PCSB and their boards of trustees can essentially have their charters revoked, resulting in closure at any time prior to their five-year review or 15-year charter term. In essence, the District's public charter schools, particularly those managed by the PCSB, function independently, are sovereign from the DCPS and other District authorities, and escape the bureaucracy of the District's public school system (Moquete 2002). Yet, in spite of this considerable autonomy, all of the District's public charter schools and their students are required to meet the same adequate yearly progress criteria outlined in the NCLB as children that attend traditional public schools.

During the 2004-2005 school year, District charter school enrollment reached an estimated 15,000 students that accounted for approximately 21% of all public school students, pre-kindergarten through grade 12 (GAO-05-490 2005). In comparison to the charter school administrations in metropolitan cities nationwide, the District of Columbia possesses the highest proportion of charter school students. Due to the assortment of options for parents seeking unique educational experiences for their children, charter school enrollment has increased and curtailed the student population in the District's traditional public schools (Haynes 2005). In the past five years, when the District's public charter schools grew the most, enrollment in traditional public schools dropped from 68,000 to 62,000 (Haynes 2005). Consequently, present DCPS Superintendent Clifford Janey has been confronted and challenged with vanquishing a two-pronged dilemma that could presumably diminish the significance and operation of traditional public schools in the District. The competition between parents seeking to enroll their children outside the District's traditional public schools through the Washington Scholarship Fund, and the escalating growth of charter schools in the nation's capital place the DCPS in a tremendous predicament for survival. It has been argued by many education reform advocates, policy analysts, educators, and politicos that competition between charter institutions and traditional public schools ultimately spawns improvement in student academic achievement, especially among African American students that are primarily in the low socioeconomic status aggregate. As Susan Schaeffler, executive director of the KIPP DC: Key Academy, inferred, the current education system as it is in the District encourages mediocrity, whereas children are now benefiting from the competition since public charter schools in the District have opened (Wolf 2005).

Since the potential implications regarding the WSF, the nation's first federally-funded school voucher program, cannot effectively be assessed until the experiment sunsets in 2009, the District's public charter movement has been recognized as placing an immediate, contiguous burden on the traditional public schools. In fact, once portrayed as a trojan horse that could destroy the District's traditional public schools, public charter schools in the nation's capital are now embraced (Lartigue 2003). Perhaps that is why five years ago, Duke Ellington School of the Arts threatened to become a charter school until it received the authority to hire teachers on its own and to control large portions of its budget (Haynes 2005). Similarly, Superintendent Janey granted the leaders at Woodrow Wilson Senior High School, the District's highest-performing comprehensive high school, more autonomy in exchange for dropping its proposal to become a charter school (Haynes 2005). Hence, the District's charter school movement could potentially, in the near future, prove itself as a viable threat to the DCPS.

Sara Mead of the Progressive Policy Institute asserts, however, that the District of Columbia is home to some of the best and worst charter schools in the country (Henorie 2005). For instance, the School for Educational Evolution and Development's (the SEED Public Charter School) first two graduating classes in 2004 and 2005 achieved a 100% acceptance rate to four-year colleges and universities (Greifner 2005). Yet, 16 of the District's public charter schools failed to meet adequate yearly progress benchmarks required by NCLB in the 2004-2005 school year, and 19 were declared "in need of improvement" (Mead 2005). Based on these disparate findings, it can be effectively argued that the District's public charter schools are not much more of an improvement, if any, than the city's traditional public schools.

Given the contention in this heated debate between the District's traditional public schools and charter schools, this chapter analyzes the perceptions of DC residents based on the following critical questions: Why are parents choosing to enroll their children in public charter schools? Will charter schools replace traditional public schools? What would be the impact on DC education if all public schools were closed? These questions comprised the survey instrument for this research.

Review of Existing Perspectives

Proponents of the charter school movement inside the District maintain that these institutions possess distinct advantages over traditional public schools largely due to the benefits of innovative teaching methodologies, avoidance of government regulations and red-tape, the ability to acquire private financial resources, and the great deal of autonomy. Yet, based on numerous and varying comparisons by researchers and policy analysts, many skeptics claim that charter schools do not help all students (NCSPE 2003). For example, during the 2004-2005 academic year, the number of students that attended Garrison Elementary School in the District shrank while enrollment in neighboring Meridian Public Charter School grew (Dobbs 2004). Garrison students, however, did better on standardized tests than their charter school counterparts (Dobbs 2004). Additionally, Cherita Whiting, a board member of the Parent-Teachers Association, acknowledged that she withdrew her son from a District charter school because she was dissatisfied with the school's academics (Haynes 2005). Furthermore, nine of the District's charter schools have closed voluntarily or had their charters revoked. Despite the recognized shortcomings and disadvantages, some parents and advocates emphasize that students attending District charter schools are better served due to personalized and unconventional approaches by faculty members, small class sizes and rigid curricula. Consequently, District public charter schools possess long wait-ing lists for enrollment (Lartigue 2003).

Although parental choice regarding District charter schools is ambigu-ous and substantively limited, due to the lack of adequate facilities and astronomical cost of real estate, most, if not all, District parents choose charter schools because they are frustrated with DCPS and desperate for better education options for their children (Mead 2006). Given that many of the District's youth require alternative solutions to their academic prob-lems, parents are increasingly enrolling their children in public charter schools because they serve students' various learning styles and offer differ-ent services for students that are not found in traditional public institu-tions (Haynes 2005). Actually, parental satisfaction for charter schools in the District is so intense that when the DCBE revoked the Village Learn-ing Center's charter in 2004 due to financial and operational problems, many parents protested because they liked the environment and alternative teaching styles (Mead 2005). The District's underprivileged children's par-ents are practically shunning the homogeneous teaching philosophy emphasized in traditional public schools in favor of progressive methodol-ogies and creative instruction that are encouraged and reinforced in char-ter institutions. Essentially, since District parents already know which traditional institutions are less desirable (Lartigue 2003), based on the abysmal performance of DCPS, charter schools effectively provide District parents an alternative means to the high-priced private schools (Mead 2005, Hendrie 2004).

In an investigation to gauge parental attitudes regarding the success of District charter institutions, Mark Schneider, Jack Buckley and Simona Kucsova's survey data in *Making the Grade: Comparing DC Charter Schools to DC Public Schools* revealed that District parents with children enrolled in charter schools rated the faculty, principals, facilities, and schools higher than the District's traditional public institutions (Schneider, Buckley and Kucsova 2003). Their investigation concluded that parental satisfaction of the District's public charter schools is largely based on their ability to influence school administrations and close interpersonal relationships maintained between teachers, parents, and administrators. Likewise, the same authors reached similar findings in *Building Social Capital in the Nation's Capital*. Specifically, their evidence suggested that charter schools in the District present an atmosphere in which parents report strong foundations of trust, respect, cooperative behavior among themselves, and between themselves and their children's teachers (Buckley, Kucsova and Schneider 2003).

Furthermore, some District parents with children that attend charter schools prefer that they learn among other students in the same socioeconomic class, race or culture. For instance, Darlene Boyd enrolled her children in Two Rivers Charter School due to the presence of other children that come from middle-class families (Hendrie 2004). Similarly, the Apple Tree Early Learning Public Charter School located in southwest Washington, DC serves a diverse student population consisting of Blacks, Whites and other races that come from upper-middle and working-class families (Mead 2005). Furthermore, the Academia Bilingue de la Comunidad (ABC) is the only dual-language middle school that suits the District's growing Latino/a population (Haynes 2005). Hence, since District charter schools seemingly draw students from their own neighborhoods, the appeal toward charter schools, in addition to other relevant factors such as contemporary learning environments and self-governance, can be attributed to shared communal values and culture.

Parental choice and satisfaction serve as catalysts for charter school growth and enrollment, as charter institutions by design are expected to inject competition into the District's public school bureaucracy for students as well as the dollars and resources that come with them (Mead 2005). Subsequently, the competition between the District's public charter schools and traditional public schools is intended to improve student academic achievement in both school systems (Mead 2005). Yet, the dynamics that affect student academic achievement, i.e. quality facilities, inexperienced faculty, relaxed or absent standards, turnover, human resources, administrative operations, and funding, generate inconclusive results for the District's charter school movement. Some education reform advocates and policy analysts indicate that there is a lack of adequate data for analysis, since charter institutions have not existed long enough to be properly examined (Wells 2004). Longitudinal comparisons are nonexistent. In essence, education reform advocates charge that charter school movements nationwide, and particularly in the District, are still considered to be in experimental stages. Moreover, Paul Hill's assertions in *Hopes, Fears, & Reality: A Balanced Look at American Charter Schools in 2005* support the foregoing presumptions. Specifically, Hill's hypothesis centers around two common and flawed assessments conducted by researchers in this controversial debate. By comparing charter school students with other children that do not attend charter schools and contrasting the different kinds of public charter schools with monolithic traditional public schools are certain to produce inconclusive results (Lake and Hill 2005). Most researchers are effectively relying on unsound comparisons using complicated tools and methodologies that demonstrate strong positives, clear negatives or, at best, weak outcomes that advance arguments for both proponents and opponents alike. Thus, when the American Federation of Teachers (AFT) examined the data from the National Assessment for Education Progress, the results of this nationwide comparison between public charter schools and conventional public schools revealed that charter school students lagged behind their traditional counterparts (Dobbs 2004). Although these conclusions were later affirmed by the Department of Education's Institute for Education Sciences, contention over the "dust up" regarding this report by charter school advocates proclaimed that the AFT arrived at its conclusion by using flawed research methodologies. Critics of AFT's analysis maintained that the research did not attempt to compare subsets of students that were similar in background and academic achievement (Carnoy, Jacobson, Mishel and Rothstein 2005). Similarly, in her rebuttal to the AFT report, Caroline Hoxby, a Harvard Economics Professor, indicated that District charter school children demonstrated a 7.4% advantage in math proficiency over their counterparts (Dobbs 2005). Essentially, Mead's presumptions in *Capital Campaign* indicate that charter schools in the District are performing roughly on par with or *slightly* better than traditional public schools can be perceived as premature (Mead 2005). Therefore, evidence suggests that it is difficult to conclude that the District's public charter schools, overall, are better than traditional public schools.

The issue of fiscal equity has also been meticulously examined by education reform advocates, policy analysts, and think-tanks. For instance, using data from FY2002-2003, the Thomas B. Fordham Institute demonstrated that a funding gap existed between District traditional and public charter institutions. Although the Fordham Institute recognized that this disparity was primarily based on expenses for capital improvements, another reason for the variance was the greater quantity of special needs students in the District's traditional public schools that qualified for additional funding than District charter institutions (Thomas B. Fordham Institute 2005). Another viewpoint in *Capital Charters*, however, acknowledges that while the PCSB and DCPS are equitable according to the baseline per-pupil formula, many students entering District charter schools require substantial medical and mental health services to compensate for the violence and dysfunction that they witness in their environments (Mead 2005). Thus, the actual spending to advance academic achievement in the two school systems is distorted. In essence, charter schools authorized by the PCSB do not have cooperative relationships with other social service agencies such as those authorized by the DCBE, and they are forced to utilize their operational funds on mental health services in an effort to improve student academic performance.

Furthermore, opponents of the District charter school movement contend that these institutions are free from accountability primarily based on the vast autonomy that they are provided. Charter schools, nevertheless, are accountable for their own success (Mickelson 1998). Thus, as stated earlier in this chapter, District charter schools that do not comply with their prescribed agreements are subject to closure. As such, Mead's predications in *Capital Campaign* recognized that charter school closures in the District, particularly those authorized by the DCBE, folded due to financial and operational problems rather than students failing to meet academic benchmarks (Mead 2005). Considering the District's political environment, however, charter school closures based on the failure to meet established academic standards have proven to be difficult. Given that most of the District's charter schools are mom-and-pop operations, exhibit safe nurturing environments and small class sizes, parental choice and influence have proven to be uncompromising, despite the academic short-comings and performance of some (Mead 2005). Thus, the DCBE and PCSB both find it difficult to close District charter schools, in which both authorizers are wedged between parental choice and closures due to low performance.

In view of the preceding perspectives, it is evident that there is not any significant, longitudinal data available to suggest that District charter school students demonstrate any significant academic improvement over traditional public school students. In fact, the results of such comparisons depend on the research and analytical methods utilized. The same data might support positive or negative conclusions depending on how they are analyzed (Lake and Hill 2005). Hence, with respect to the significance that parental choice and satisfaction evinces in the District's charter school movement, it can be effectively argued that until both authorizers close charter schools for poor academic achievement rather than fiscal and oper-ational failure, District charter institutions have the potential to replicate the academic performance of DCPS students. In essence, the evidence pre-sented thus far indicates that the expansion of public charter schools does not pose a significant, viable and immediate threat to DCPS. At best, pub-lic charter schools in the District will equally co-exist with their counter-parts.

Data Analysis

In order to determine if the evidence and preceding suppositions correlate with the perspectives of District residents, a random telephone survey was conducted from February through April of 2006. Accordingly, District residents were asked the questions noted earlier in the introduction section of this chapter. The following discussion analyzes the findings of this sur-vey.

As demonstrated in Table 1, a preponderance of the survey respondents (85%) indicated that they believe DC parents choose to enroll their children in District public charter schools based on the quality of education that they provide or their dissatisfaction with DCPS and its bureaucracy. Conversely, a small proportion of survey respondents indicated that safety reasons such as crime and violence, and small class sizes were the primary motivations for choosing to enroll their children in public charter schools. Some respondents did not know, were unsure what public charter schools are, or failed to respond to the question.

Table 1: Why do you think some DC parents choose to enroll their children in public charter schools? (N=220)

Response	N	%
Better Quality of Education	138	62.7
Dissatisfied with DCPS/Bureaucracy	49	22.3
Don't know	13	5.9
Small class size	8	3.6
Safety Reasons	5	2.3
Not sure of what a public charter schools are	5	2.3
No response	1	0.9

Table 2 reveals that greater than three-fourths of the respondents did not believe public charter schools will replace the District's traditional public schools. In contrast, some respondents believed that charters will succeed the District's traditional public schools, while other respondents failed to provide an indication. In essence, these respondents did not know if DC's public charter schools would replace traditional public schools.

Table 3 demonstrates that if all the District's traditional public schools were closed, the greatest impact would affect poor and minority children, according to the respondents. Almost half of the survey respondents indicated that in the event of such closure, the District's poor and minority children will not have access to education, in which DC's children from wealthy parents would only have access to education, specifically, private schools. Furthermore, a significant proportion of survey respondents did not know or speculated what the impact on DC education would be if all traditional public schools were closed. Some respondents indicated that the quality of DC education would improve, while others stated that DC's traditional public schools will not close despite the growth of public charter schools. As noted, other replies varied. Eight respondents chose not to answer the question.

Table 2: Do you think DC public charter schools will replace traditional public schools? (N=220)

Response	N	%
No	171	77.7
Don't know	25	11.4
Yes	20	9.1
No response	4	1.8

Table 3: What would be the impact on DC education if all traditional public schools were closed? (N=220)

Response	N	%
Poor & Minority children won't have access to education/ Only wealthy would have access to education	102	46.4
Don't know	46	20.9
Quality of DC education would improve	14	6.4
DC's traditional public schools won't close	14	6.4
Increase in crime/poverty/unemployment	8	3.6
DC children would be forced to be home schooled/attend schools in MD or VA/attend charter or private schools	8	3.6
No response	8	3.6
Number of charter schools would increase	6	2.7
New education system would be created	6	2.7
Quality of DC education would decline	3	1.4

Less accountability and consistency in DC schools	2	0.9
Charter schools and private schools would become subsidized federal programs	1	0.5
Signify DC public schools are a failure	1	0.5
No impact at all	1	0.5

Conclusion and Recommendations

By comparing the existing perceptions on the District's public charter schools with the preceding survey results, it is easy to conclude that DC residents' responses confirmed the suppositions noted earlier in this chapter. A significant proportion of District parents are choosing to enroll their children in public charter schools because they *presumably* offer a better quality education, are displeased with the DCPS and its governance, and prefer small class sizes and safer educational environments. The survey results, however, *imply* a disconnection between DC residents' perceptions of DC public charter schools and their actual performance. Subsequently, this inference raises three fundamental research questions for future investigation: (1) Would District parents choose to enroll their children in DC public charter schools if they were fully aware that, overall, charter schools in the nation's capital have not demonstrated a significant improvement, if any, over traditional public schools? (2) If DC parents were aware of these nominal, yet sporadic, improvements, would they still choose to enroll their children in public charter schools? (3) If so, what would be their reasons?

Given the growth of public charter schools inside the District, it is evident that they pose a threat to DCPS' public schools. The significance, urgency and achievability of the District's public charter school impositions, however, have yet to be determined. Furthermore, since most education reformists and parents believe that the District's public charter schools will coexist with traditional public schools, to what degree and for how long?

Perhaps Superintendent Janey has found a way for DCPS to simultaneously subsist by recently collaborating with one of the nation's most respected and successful public charter school organizations, the Knowledge Is Power Program (KIPP). Under this novel strategy to avoid the remote possibility of DCPS' demise, Janey reached an agreement with KIPP officials to house both schools in one facility, in which students from Scott Montgomery Elementary that pass the fourth grade would enroll in the KIPP organization's middle school (Haynes 2006). In essence, Janey's collaboration with KIPP will effectively serve as an unprecedented feeder program. It is the first of its kind that could result in monumental success or colossal failure and, perchance, the demise of DCPS (Haynes 2006).

Without considering the success or failure of Janey's recent accord with KIPP, District education officials hopefully recognize that innovation and creativity are imperative to the survival and success of DCPS. The school system can ill afford for the District's 51 public charter schools to keep siphoning off its students every school year. If District parents continue enrolling their children in public charter schools, the closure of DCPS' traditional public schools have great potential to become a grim reality. This occurrence would inflict tremendous harm on the city's poor and minority children. Hence, it is essential that Janey continuously work with the District's public charter schools rather than against them as some propose (Mead 2005).

To impede the incessant flow of students departing the District's traditional public schools and their closure altogether, DCPS officials and Superintendent Janey must adopt some of the same policies and practices that have proven to be successful in District charter schools. For instance, rather than *recommending* that District teachers should establish positive relationships with parents, Janey's administration should require constructing and preserving interpersonal relationships as school policy. Granted, implementing this measure is limited primarily because it does not guarantee reciprocal cooperation or full parental participation. This form of cooperative behavior, however, is embraced, pervasive and, most importantly, successful in the District's public charter schools. Hence, this action would demonstrate a concerted effort on behalf of DCPS officials and Janey and, hopefully, improve parental attitudes, trust and satisfaction toward principals, teachers, and administrators.

The City Council, school board members, DCPS officials and Janey should not only consider consolidating or closing some facilities due to their low enrollments; they should shut down traditional public schools *themselves* solely for failing to meet required academic standards in spite of NCLB's ramifications. Furthermore, the successful practices of the District's high performing traditional public schools as well as flourishing charter schools should be replicated in those institutions that are failing. As noted earlier in the introduction section of this chapter, Janey extended greater autonomy to Duke Ellington School of the Arts and Woodrow Wilson Senior High School. Thus, as an incentive to improve and sustain superior academic achievement in unavailing schools, Janey's decision established precedence for others to follow and could be compelled to proffer commensurate levels of independence and reduced oversight.

Whether the District's parents and children are aware or oblivious to the actions of DCPS, Superintendent Janey's decisions, for all intents and purposes, have a substantial impact on their future. Hopefully, for their sake, Janey's motivation and advancements will prove to be beneficial. Otherwise, thousands of the District's children, specifically Blacks, Hispanics and those in the low socioeconomic aggregate, will be left in dire straits.

3

Public Schools

◆

Autumn Saxton-Ross

Introduction

Like the dispute over "Home Rule" and self-governance within the District of Columbia's political system, DC's Public Schools (DCPS) system has a similar history with the governance and accountability of its schools. In early 2000, the City Council and the Mayor disagreed in how to structure the School Board—whether its members should be appointed by the mayor, or consist of a fully elected panel. This issue arose on the heels of the 1996 woes when the financial control board (which at one time oversaw the city's operations) stripped the elected school board of most of its powers because of continuous deficits and overspending (Gewertz 2000). In February of 2004, Mayor Anthony Williams announced his plan to take over the school system which met with opposition from the school board and city council, but surprised support from many District residents (Reid 2004).

At the present time, DC's public schools are governed by the DC Board of Education, the official policy-making body for education related issues, where five of its members are elected, four appointed by the Mayor, with the remaining two seats filled by non-voting student members (DC for Democracy 2006). Every fiscal year as the school system requests funding, the Mayor's office submits this budget to the City Council, which then either approves or rejects the budget, or offers amendments. With major disagreements amongst the District's elected officials in the City Council,

School Board, or the appointees, one thing is certain—DCPS faces immense challenges from low performance to truancy to poor facilities, ultimately affecting the quality of the District's education.

Currently, the DCPS system educates approximately 65,000 students, with over half of its student population (39,000) attending elementary schools. The student population is a racially condensed community when compared to the city's overall population, with a disproportionate number of White children enrolled in private schools (DC for Democracy, 2006). Sixty percent of DC's residents are Black, 29% are White, whereas 85% of the schools' children are Black, with only 5% being White. In 1998, the US Army Corps of Engineers, who historically have been in charge of major construction and facility assessment of DCPS, found that 70% of DCPS facilities were in poor physical condition (General Accounting Office [GAO] 2002).

There are 167 schools and learning centers within DC (147 currently in use by DCPS), some built before 1900 (DC for Democracy 2006). The majority of the District's public school facilities are over 65 years old and in complete disrepair from falling ceilings, malfunctioning heating, non-existent cooling systems, and broken boilers to faulty electrical systems that cannot support today's technological needs for the classrooms. As a result of the Army Corps' assessments, lawsuits by parent and student advocacy groups, and escalating media coverage of the deplorable educational environment, DCPS submitted and subsequently passed the Facility Master Plan in 2002. This initiative, based on an assessment of the system's current facility needs, delineated a 15-year plan to modernize all school facilities in need in a series of stages. Even after an initial push within the first two years of the plan, the results have been decreased improvements and continuous under-funding by the Mayor (0% for fiscal years 2008 and 2009) and a 44% decrease for 2006 (Cooper 2002). Once again, parents, communities and advocacy groups have mobilized on the side of DC's children's need for a modern, healthy and safe learning environment (DC for Democracy 2006).

Accepted by the DC City Council on March 7, 2006, the School Construction and Modernization Trust Fund proposed by Council members

Kathy Patterson and Jack Evens was established as a segregated special revenue fund of the government of the District of Columbia requiring the Chief Financial Officer to deposit any taxes and fees designated by law (revenues from development partnerships and any federal funds or grants that may be used for the purposes of the fund) for DC school modernization and construction. The monies directed into this fund will be used to bring any existing school up to today's standards set by DCPS and building codes, and can include partial or complete demolition, new construction, rehabilitation of existing facilities or any combination (DC Modernization Fund Campaign 2006). This fund is the first of its type separating funds specifically for facility improvement and construction, raising funds from the broader business community, the hotel and tourism industry, and increases in the commercial real estate and cigarette tax, boasting possible revenues between two and half to three billion dollars over the next 15 years (Newswire 12/1/2005).

This set aside fund will be managed by a five-member Board of Directors: two appointed by the Board of Education, one by the Mayor, and the final by the City Council, all of whom must be District residents. The Board of Directors is responsible for the selection of firms to review the public real estate portfolio and prepare business studies for the development and identification of public and private partnerships. With direction from the Board of Education, the Board of Directors must establish development partnerships in which property or land owned by the Board of Education is sold or leased for development. The monies deposited into this fund may be used for the solicitation of proposals, the purchase of school sites and improvements, the building and or purchase, furnishing and equipping of a school building, repair or improvement of a school building or site and the associated architectural, engineering, consulting, demolition and legal costs (DC School Construction and Modernization Trust Fund Establishment Act 2005).

One of the reasons for the lack of facilities upkeep within the District is that, historically, there has been a lack of stable funding at a level high enough to improve the system's aging buildings, where this bill's most prominent feature addresses this issue—it provides dedicated revenue that can only be used for facility improvements (Editorial, *Washington Post* 2005 A20). The proposition behind the modernization of schools is that when students are surrounded by dilapidated buildings with broken windows or crumbling walls and ceilings, entire wings off limits, or new computers that can't be used unless the classroom lights are off, not only is their health in jeopardy, but the emphasis on learning becomes secondary. Through an observation of Washington, DC's residents' beliefs of this bill, The School Construction and Modernization Trust Fund Act of 2005, this chapter examines the perceptions of its passing, utility and distribution of the funds through the eight wards of Washington, DC.

When attempting to examine Washington DC's education system in the present, or historically, there are very few existing works. Data for this study were collected using random telephone interviews of Washington, DC residents with an instrument developed by the researcher. Participants were asked a series of three questions that focused on DC residents' perceptions of key educational issues, specifically their knowledge of the City Council's newly passed law—the School Construction and Modernization Trust Fund. The data collected from the telephone interviews were analyzed using frequency distributions and percentages. The purpose of this chapter is not to confirm relationships or to test hypothesis, but to describe the issues, concerns and perceptions of DC residents by asking the following questions:

1. Did you know that the City Council passed legislation for the School Construction and Modernization Trust Fund?

2. Do you think building new schools will improve the education of the District's children?

3. Do you think the funds will be distributed equally among the wards?

Review of Existing Works

Soon after the preliminary approval of this bill, *The Washington Post* sponsored a live chat with the Chief Business Operations Officer of DCPS,

Thomas Brady, who is responsible for the implementation of the strategic plan for overall operations of the District, including budget planning and administration, management of facilities management, contracts, realty and the federal grants program. Within this conversation, various, often opposing, opinions on the relationships between new facilities, education and academic success were expressed, embodying the many opinions of community members, parents and media. This chapter reviews some of these perspectives, beginning with how Washington DC's school facilities came to be in their present condition, national views and trends on school modernization, and common sources of funding for these programs.

When a discussion begins on academic success and the current school system in Washington, DC, quite often someone states that DC spends the most amount of money per pupil than any other system in the area. Contrary to the majority opinion, DC does not spend the most per student. As of FY2006, DCPS budgeted $11,498 per student, thousands less than Arlington ($16,051) and Alexandria ($15,389) in Virginia, and Montgomery County ($12,023) in Maryland, and slightly more than Fairfax, Virginia ($11,342) and Prince George's County, Maryland ($8,909) (DC Modernization Fund Campaign 2006). Unknown to the proponents of this perspective are three very important determinants of how effective school budgets are: (1) the proportion of students from low-income households, (2) inflation, and (3) funding allocation for facilities and maintenance.

In school systems that have a disproportionate number of students from low-income families, it is generally thought that these systems require greater education resources and money than those with students from higher income households (DC Modernization Fund Campaign 2006). Over half of DCPS' student population (69.7%) comes from low-income households, the highest percentage in the metropolitan area, compared to 19.1% in Fairfax and 36.1% in Arlington. Progressively over the past 10 years, just like other inner city school districts, budgets have increased significantly when examining the numbers alone; but when taking into account inflation, these increases were absorbed by 20.8%, reflecting the dollar's true purchasing power (US Census Bureau 2004). When examining these budgets using the Consumer Price Index (CPI), which includes cost of living increases, pay raises, utilities, security, basic services and the insufficient special education program (which, because of lack of facilities within the District, requires the system to cover out-of-state tuition, legal fees and transportation of many students with special needs), the amount of money per pupil becomes apparently inadequate.

Prior to the recent Facilities Master Plan, another existed, written in 1967 by the General Services Administration which managed Washington, DC's buildings. Over the past four decades, the inconsistent rule of the city between the federal government and city administrators echoed in the maintenance of school facilities. During this time, new buildings were built, but the needed large scale renovations of most buildings were limited to 'patch-up' jobs—when needing to replace the HVAC system, because of lack of funds, new plaster was put up and painted, masking the underlying infrastructure damage (DC School Modernization Campaign 2006). The cost of major and minor renovations and facility upkeep is included in the per-student budget costs; and when examining the already beleaguered budget needs within the District, it is easy to see how the schools got so bad. Before the arrival of the new superintendent, DCPS allocated $1.10 per square foot for maintenance and repairs, when the standard was at $2.20, assuming that regular maintenance and repair periodically occurred (DC School Modernization Campaign 2006). As of 2006, DCPS has increased this allocation to $1.76 (Brady 2006), an improvement but a far cry from what is needed for so many neglected facilities.

To modernize schools, the school system planned to build a new school, demolish an old one, or completely renovate an existing school (GAO 2002). Prior to the acceptance of the Facilities Master Plan in 2000, in 1998, DCPS and the Army Corps of Engineers entered into an agreement for engineering and construction, taking the lead in the projects requiring the replacement of major building systems like boilers, roofs and windows (GAO 2002). According to this plan, $1.3 billion was allocated for the modernization of 10 schools a year over 10-15 years. But, in late 2001, this plan was revised, and it was found that to accomplish these goals, significantly more money (approximately $150 million per year) was needed, reflecting better (yet higher) construction costs and community needs for special facilities (GAO 2002). In March of 2002, the Chief Financial Officer of Washington, DC advised the school system that due to its debt and limited borrowing capacity, it must complete the needs within the approved budget (Cooper 2002), lengthening the time of the plan which results in even more budget increases.

Eight reports from the General Accounting Office (GAO) have been issued dealing with the cost of repairing and renovating the nation's aging school buildings, suggesting a minimum of $11 billion to a maximum of $112 billion needed (CRS 2003). According to the National Center for Education Statistics (NCES), three-quarters of the nation's schools need funding to bring their buildings into a 'good overall condition,' where these unmet needs for construction and renovation top an estimated $127 billion. The Department of Education states that the average age of public school facilities is estimated at 42 years, an age when buildings begin to deteriorate. The age, however, is somewhat less important than the facility's history of maintenance and repair (NCES 2000). Many schools are in a state of disrepair because, often, district officials (due to insufficient funds) continually defer maintenance and repair. Without regular upkeep, building problems progressively get worse, continually increasing the cost of maintaining buildings.

The General Accounting Office (GAO) in 1995 reported that 14 million of the nation's students attended schools that were in need of serious repairs, that one-third of both elementary and secondary schools reported having at least one entire building in need of extensive repairs, and that 60 percent of schools reported having at least one building feature (roof, HVAC system, etc.) needing repair, overhaul or replacement. The features in need most, like the heating/air conditioning systems, ventilation, plumbing, windows and doors, caused 41% of the schools to report poor energy efficiency, adding additional costs to an already burdened system. At least 50 percent of schools reported unsatisfactory environmental conditions, many of which violate federal mandates (like lead and asbestos exposure). This neglect makes it impossible for many school facilities to meet proposed system, state and federal technology goals, decreasing student potential and contributing to increases in the "digital divide."

In examining the information provided, the condition of the nation's schools vary widely with many in disrepair or exceptional condition, where most fall somewhere in the middle (NCES 2000). These variations occur by location or characteristics of the local school community, with the largest portion of schools reporting deplorable conditions in central cities serving a population of at least 50 percent minority or 70 percent poor, or those in rural areas (GAO 1996). These reports have raised issues, concerns, and often law suits, as to the effects of dilapidated buildings on teaching and learning, especially when some conditions raise concerns about the health and safety of students and teachers.

Funding for public education is a combination of state and local appropriations and some federal funds. Quite often, the determining factor of school facility condition and repair is the local revenue, drawn by property tax base. These variations in tax base contribute to the disparities observed in funding. The majority of funding for school construction is provided indirectly from federal support by exempting the interest on state and local governmental bonds from federal income taxes and other tax code provisions (CRS). Additional direct funding can be provided when included in public laws (like the $1.2 billion for emergency school renovation and repair in P.L. 107-554 or the provisions included in the No Child Left Behind Act) (CRS 2001).

Traditionally, renovations were funded from either bonds whose interest payments are included in taxable income, called taxable bonds, or through bonds whose interest payment is not included in federal taxable income, referred to as tax-exempt bonds (CRS 2001). As more reports were released, and the National Center for Education Statistics projected that an estimated $127 billion was needed to repair or upgrade school facilities (US Department of Education 1999), Congress passed legislation which lowered the cost of borrowing for some school districts through Qualified Zone Academy Bonds (QZAB). These bonds allow state education departments or local school districts to receive zero interest rates of school renovation loans. In addition, the lender is given tax credits against federal income taxes. This program continued for four years and allocated over $1.6 billion (CRS 2001).

When examining Washington, DC's school modernization issues within the context of national school facility improvements, Washington, DC is no different from any other district that is composed primarily of minority and/or poor populations. From these perspectives, when looking for resolutions to inadequate school building funding, parents, communities and policy makers must account not only for inflation when amassing budgets, but also keep districts from draining facility maintenance funds when dollars come up short.

Data Analysis

The results of the first question (Table 1) show that the majority of respondents (61%) did not know that the DC City Council had passed the School Construction and Modernization Trust Fund. Surprisingly, only 37% of DC residents interviewed for this research knew of the passing of this law. Greater knowledge about this bill was expected because of the widespread media coverage and the innovative source of funds. Washington, DC, because of the federal government (its interns and fellows), colleges, universities, and young childless professionals, is considered to have a large transient population. With this type of population, it is quite possible that local issues and concerns have much less precedence because of "temporary residence." This could explain the high percentage of residents that were not aware of this law.

Table 1: Did you know that the City Council passed legislation for the School Construction and Modernization Trust Fund? (N=220)

Response	N	%
No	135	61
Yes	82	37

| Don't know | 1 | 1 |
| No response | 2 | 1 |

When respondents were asked if they believed that new schools would improve the education of DC's children (Table 2), 42% agreed, whereas 33% disagreed. When examining the responses to obtain a better under-standing of themes beyond basic yes and no answers, two perceptions emerged. Both generally agreed that new buildings/facilities had an impact in improving education, where the first consisted of respondents, (11%), who believed that new buildings fostered a better learning environment and nine percent agreed that it was a start, but thought that other resources, like better curricula or teachers, would have a greater impact to improve education. This perception reflects a major issue determining aca-demic success in DCPS. Like the shifts in governmental control within the city, the school system experienced continuous turnovers in its leadership; with each new superintendent, new models and reforms were introduced. With this, many initiatives were not formally assessed, evaluated, or con-sistently used with a clear agenda to produce reliable results (Gibson 2000). The direct result of this is inconsistent educational models and var-ied teacher requirements affecting academic success.

Table 2: Do you think building new schools will improve the education of the District's children? (N=220)

Response	N	%
Yes	93	42
No	73	33
Fosters a better learning environment	24	11
A start, need better curricula or teachers	19	9
Don't know	6	3

Table 3: Do you think the funds will be distributed equally among the wards? (N=220)

Response	N	%
No	154	70
No, Race/Class	17	8
Don't know	16	7
Should be according to need	12	6
No, Politics	10	5
Yes	10	5
No Response	1	0.5

In addition to the four large quadrants of Washington, DC (Northwest, Northeast, Southwest and Southeast), the city is further divided into eight wards (the equivalent to districts in other cities). The elementary, middle and high schools within DCPS are spread out over these wards, with the majority of children residing in Wards 7 and 8. These two wards also happen to have the smallest percentages of White residents and large numbers of residents living at or below poverty. From Table 3, when asked if the funds generated and channeled to the Modernization Fund would be equally distributed among the eight wards within the District, 70 percent responded no, in that they did not believe that the money from the fund would be distributed equally, as opposed to five percent responding yes, believing that the money would be equally distributed between the wards. In addition to the large percentage of those that disagreed, eight percent responded no, specifically citing race and class issues as reasons why monies will not be distributed equally. Similarly, an additional five percent responded no, citing politics as the reason why monies would not be distributed equally. The remaining six percent believed that the money should be distributed according to each individual ward's needs—those with the most schools in disrepair securing more money.

Conclusion and Recommendations

Many believe and studies have shown that students who attend class in clean, safe, modern buildings do better in class while receiving a message about their self-worth, unlike those who attend overcrowded and run-down schools (NCES 1999). But in some studies, the influence of school conditions on academic achievement has been linked more to cosmetic improvements than structural and mechanical repairs (NCES 1999). Within these studies, many of the underlying social and economic conditions are not included. Quite often, when schools are in disrepair, it is a function of the surrounding community and its tax base. Schools in poor condition most likely lack other important resources that may have a more direct impact on academic success like quality teachers, parental involvement, challenging curricula and textbooks. It is likely that these resources may explain the observed differences in student achievement, and not just the school's physical characteristics (NCES 1999). In no way should the inconsistent findings of direct relationships between building conditions and academic achievement minimize the decades of neglect observed in many central cities and rural school districts.

Based on these findings, there are several recommendations that can be made to address the deplorable conditions of many of our nation's schools, on the federal, state and local level. First, there must be a re-organization of school budgets. Quite often, when money is lacking for educational necessities, the facility and maintenance budget is used as an overflow fund—its funds redirected for other uses. Not unlike Washington, DC's new School Modernization Trust Fund, there must be funds set aside for the sole purpose of preserving, maintaining and repairing existing buildings. Also, the allocation of educational funding must be derived with inflation in mind, using the Consumer Price Index (CPI). This will allow each section within the educational system to receive adequate monetary amounts, decreasing the likelihood of under-funding and improving the overall functionality of the educational system. Finally, specifically in Washington, DC, once the Trust Fund accumulates adequate funds, the initiation of projects must be rotated by individual Wards, beginning with those that have the most children attending public schools and those with the most buildings in need of repairs.

Washington, DC is not alone in its aging school facilities, or lack of funds for renovations and repairs. This nationwide issue must be put in the forefront of community activism, state and federal initiatives. As seen in the results of the present study, issues that surround why buildings are dilapidated like politically charged environments, the socioeconomic issues of race, class and income, and the fundamental building blocks of success, like qualified teachers, innovative and consistent curricula and educational resources, must be addressed. Academic success cannot be attributed to a single source; it is a combination of parental involvement, adequate resources, teacher qualifications and experience. All of these are a result of local and state governments improving education for all students, regardless of location, to be placed at the forefront, and not just political rhetoric.

4

Colleges and Universities

◆

Vernese Edghill

Introduction

This chapter explores District of Columbia (DC) residents' perceptions about the District of Columbia Tuition Assistance Grant (DCTAG) program, the program's impact on DC resident's enrollment in DC colleges and universities, as well as its influence on racial diversity amongst student enrollment. To better understand this issue, this chapter provides an in-depth examination of the DCTAG, DC colleges and universities student body, along with the DC residents' perceptions of the tuition assistance program, and how this program may or may not influence DC high school students' decision to attend DC colleges and universities.

Throughout the United States, there are thousands of private and public colleges and universities that offer a variety of educational opportunities. All colleges and universities have independent governing boards of trustees and presidents who report to their boards. All institutions have professional administrators and faculty who are responsible for the academic and student life of all students enrolled. However, few colleges in the Untied States are tuition free, which indicates that most students must be able to afford the cost of or have access to student aid to pay for the colleges or universities they wish to attend. To assist with access to higher education, however, the District of Columbia offers tuition assistance to DC residents to attend colleges and universities that participate in a tuition assistance program.

According the State Education Office, the DC Tuition Assistance Program was established in 1999 through the District of Columbia College Access Act (PL106-98). It allows the Mayor of the District to award grants to children of DC residents who wish to attend public institutions of higher learning in the surrounding states. These grants pay the difference between in-state and out-of-state tuition and fees for part-time and full-time students. Each award is not to exceed $10,000 per year and should not exceed $50,000 over time. Prior to 2002, children of diplomats were eligible for assistance. An amendment was passed, however, that no longer allows children of diplomats to be eligible for this program (www.dc.gov/seo).

In 2002, the act was amended by the College Access Improvement Act to include access to private historically black colleges and universities (HBCUs) throughout the country. Students do need to attend college within three years of graduation or must have graduated after January 1, 1998. Prior to the College Access Improvement Act amendment, only students with high school diplomas were eligible for assistance. Currently, this act also offers assistance to students with GEDs, as long as they can prove DC residency (www.dc.gov/seo).

In December of 2004, the *Congressional Quarterly* reported that Tom Davis (R-VA), House of Government Reform Committee Chairman, announced that the US House of Representatives approved the extension of the H.R. 4012 legislation, District of Columbia College Access Program, for two more years. The legislation was introduced jointly by Chairman Davis and Congresswoman Eleanor Holmes Norton (D-DC) to maintain the Tuition Assistance Grants (TAG) program which was formerly established in 1999. This program was initially developed to fulfill two strategic goals for city redevelopment: (1) the District did not have a state university system for high school students to attend, and this program would level the playing field for DC high school graduates by allowing them to attend colleges and universities around the country at in-State tuition prices; (2) the program's purpose was to deter tax paying families in the District from moving to surrounding states by providing them with in-state tuition in neighboring states, thereby stabilizing the District's tax revenue (Congressional Quarterly 2004).

Tom Davis argued that this program has been a key component of the District's revitalization. He also noted that the District's high school graduates matriculating to college has increased 28%, higher than the national average increase of 5%. He further reported that high school students receiving aid surveyed indicated that the grants available through this program influenced their decisions to attend college and was a key factor in their decisions to attend college, providing access to a better education and better life for many DC students (Congressional Quarterly 2004).

The DCTAG program offers students a variety of educational opportunities outside of the District, but the schools in the District should not be overlooked. There are approximately 16 four-year and two-year private and two public accredited tuition based colleges and universities in the District (Chronicle of Higher Education 2005). The University of the District of Columbia and Howard University are the only two predominantly Black universities. However, the University of the District of Columbia (UDC) is the District's only entirely public college. Many of the other colleges and universities receive federal funds (e.g., Howard, Georgetown, American) but are still considered private institutions.

Although many colleges and universities were founded by religious organizations, only Georgetown University and Catholic University still have a major Jesuit afflation. The 16 schools offer a variety of educational resources and many different types of undergraduate and graduate programs. Some of the schools have specific missions and cater to students interested in learning a specific skill or trade or have certain learning styles. For example, Gallaudet University is specifically for the deaf community, Dudley Beauty College is for students interested in Cosmetology, and students interested in art, art history and fashion design can attend The Corcoran College of Art and Design.

This chapter is restricted to the examination of six of the largest universities in the District, which include American University, Catholic University, George Washington University, Georgetown University, Howard University, and the University of the District of Columbia. This chapter is significant because it provides data on DC residents' awareness of the tuition assistance program. It also attempts to answer the following questions: (1) How might the DC tuition assistance program increase racial diversity in DC colleges and universities? (2) Are more DC residents attending DC colleges and universities because of the DC tuition assistance program?

This survey began March 1, 2006 and ran until April 10, 2006. Data were collected by utilizing a four-question item telephone survey instrument with a sample size of 220 DC residents. They were asked about their perceptions of the DC Tuition Assistance Program. Of the 220 participants, some respondents did not answer all four questions; therefore, the response rate for each question varies and indicated in Tables 1-4 in this study.

To better understand this issue, the data were analyzed using descriptive statistics (frequency distributions and percentages) generated by the Statistical Package for the Social Sciences (SPSS). The types of questions asked focused on (a) residents' awareness of the program, (b) residents' perceptions about whether the DCTAG program increases racial diversity in DC colleges and universities, and (c) finally if they believe DC colleges and universities' enrollments would increase as a result of the DCTAG program. The actual questioned asked were as follows:

1. What do you know about the DC Tuition Assistance Program?

2. How did you learn about the DC Tuition Assistance Program?

3. Do you think the DC Tuition Assistance Program will increase diversity in DC colleges and universities?

4. Are more DC residents attending DC colleges and universities because of the DC Tuition Assistance Program?

Review of Available Perspectives

There is a large body of perspectives on the access, recruitment and retention of students to higher education. The following review of available perspectives provides an understanding of a sample of the literature available on this topic.

DCTAG Program

The *Congressional Quarterly* reported, in 2004, that 6,500 students have received tuition assistance since the year 2000. DCTAG also, in 2001, amended the legislation to approve funding for up to $2,500 for DC high school students to attend private colleges and universities in surrounding counties around the District and private Historically Black Colleges and Universities throughout the country. This amendment was added to the existing legislation that awarded $10,000 per year to students wanting to enroll in public institutions in other states (Congressional Quarterly 2004).

In March of 2006, the Congress called for a reauthorization of the DC Tuition Assistance Grant Program of 1999 for five more years. Eleanor Holmes Norton stated that this legislation far exceeded everyone's expectations. Mayor Anthony Williams, Mayor of the District of Columbia, supported this reauthorization by noting the 35 percent increase in the number of DC students attending college and the approximately 5,000 students who were receiving funding in the 2005-2006 school year (Roll Call 2006).

Also in March of 2006, the States News Service reported that the 2006 reauthorization of the DCTAG program called for a proposed $35 million for the 2007 fiscal year with a five-year extension. On March 9, 2006, the State News Service also reported that the House Committee on Government Reform unanimously approved this additional five years of funding for the DCTAG (State News Service 2006).

DC Colleges and Universities

In an article entitled the "District Of Columbia," Paul Fain provided the District's demographics. Of a population of 553,523, 10% of the city's population is made up of people aged 18 to 24 years old, and the overall racial distribution of the city includes 0.3% Native American, 3.1 Asian, 58.8% Black, 0.1% Pacific Islander, 36.2% White, Hispanic and those counted under other races make up 1.4%. The largest percentage of the population at 22.9% has obtained a graduate or professional degree, and the second highest has earned at least a bachelor's degree, with a 6% high school drop out rate; approximately17.8% speak languages other than English; the per-capita income was $51,803 in 2005; and the poverty rate is 16.9% (Chronicle of Higher Education 2005).

Overall, there is a total of 91,014 students enrolled at the 16 colleges and universities in the District. Of these, over 54,000 are enrolled as undergraduates and over 26,000 are pursuing graduate education. The overall racial profile of the students is as follows: 250 is Native American, 6,081 are Asian, 28,335 are Black, 4,000 are Hispanic, 43,972 are White, and 8,326 are foreign students. About 86% of minority students are enrolled in public four-year institutions, and 39.7% are enrolled at private four-year institutions. In 2002, 29% of the District residents who were freshmen that year enrolled in District of Columbia institutions of higher education. The average SAT score of these District residents was 965, which reflects 77% of the District's high school seniors' scores (Chronicle of Higher Education 2005).

American University was charted by an Act of Congress in 1893. In 1914, it admitted four women for the first time; and in 1937, it was one of the first White universities in the country to admit Black students. Currently, American enrolls over 5,000 undergraduate students from across the United States. Approximately 1,203 freshmen are enrolled each year, with a male/female ratio of 35/65, and 17% of the freshmen class is made up of minority students. The average cost of tuition is $27,552 (www.american.edu).

Howard University was founded in 1867 as a school to educate freed Africans. It is one of two historically black universities in Washington, DC. Howard accepts over 4,000 of the 8,000 undergraduate student applicants. Students who enrolled in fall 2005 totaled 1,453 (first-time college students). Approximately 52% of the student body is from the Mid-Atlantic region, 23% of the students come from the South, 12% from the Mid-West, 10% from the West coast, and 3% from the New England states. The majority of the students from the Mid-Atlantic region come from Maryland. Tuition for undergraduates is $10,840 and is higher for students enrolled in its graduate and professional schools. During the 2003-2004 school year, both graduate and undergraduate students who received financial aid totaled 11,560 (www.howard.edu).

George Washington University is considered a mid-sized institution that enrolls 9,700 full-time undergraduates. The most recent freshmen applicant pool was made up of 20,000 students, of which only 2,400 were admitted. About 65% of each freshman class is amongst the top 10% of its high school class with average SAT scores of 1,260 to 1,410. George Washington University's demographic profile is as follows: 6% Black and Hispanic, 10% Asian, less than 1% Native American, 63% White, 4% international students. Most of the students come from the Mid-Atlantic region (44%), 17% from the New England states, 13% from the West and Northwest, 12% from the Southwest, 10% from the Central United States, and 4% from outside the United States (www.gwu.edu).

Georgetown University was founded in 1789 and is the oldest Catholic University with an undergraduate applicant pool of 15,285 students: 3,3286 are generally admitted, and 1,530 enroll. Like most of the other schools focused on in this chapter, the largest number of students comes from the Mid-Atlantis states (395). There are approximately 53.9% females and 46.1% males in the 2005-2006 freshman class. Nearly 22% of Georgetown's student population is from a minority ethnic background, and the 2005-2006 freshman class comprised of 25% students from minority ethnic backgrounds. The overall racial diversity of the student population is 6.7% Black, 9.1% Asian and 5.8% Hispanic. Georgetown is second only to Howard in graduating the largest number of African American lawyers from its Law School. The tuition is $31,000 for undergraduates and slightly less for graduate school (www.georgetwon.edu).

Catholic University was founded in 1887 as a graduate and research center and in 1904 established an undergraduate program. It is a Jesuit institution which has an average undergraduate enrollment of 3,053 and a graduate enrollment of 3, 077. Although the university accepts and welcomes students from all faiths, the majority of the undergraduates (84%) are Catholic and 59% of its graduate students are also Catholic. Like many of the other institutions, 58% of the school's student population is from the Mid-Atlantic region and the second largest population of students comes from the South. Undergraduate and some of the graduate tuitions are $24,800 per year, but the tuitions of the other graduate and professional schools range from $16,000 to $30,000 per year. Eighty-one percent of the undergraduates and 97% of the first-time, full-time undergraduates receive financial aid, which represents $26.4 million of the school's operating budget, $46.9 million of which comes from the federal budget, and $2.7 million of which comes from university endowed scholarships (www.cua.edu/).

The University of the District of Columbia (UDC) is the only other HBCU in the District. It was founded in 1974 as the only public institution in the District after combining three other historically black schools of higher leaning. UDC's historical mission has been to serve the community and make higher education affordable to District of Columbia residents (www.udc.edu).

In the early 1900s, there were Normal schools for Blacks which were eventually named District's Teachers College. This college was established for Blacks interested in becoming teachers. However, if one wanted to pursue a trade or technical skill, but were poor and Black, there were no institutions accessible to him/her. After years of lobbying, President John F. Kennedy in 1963 commissioned a study of the District's higher education needs. One of the findings in the report gave rise to the need to establish a comprehensive public institution of higher learning in the District. In 1966, the Public Education Act was passed, and two schools were created—the Federal City College and the Washington Technical Institute. These schools opened their doors in 1968, and students were accepted through a lottery system. After years of functioning as three separate entities, the Boards of Trustees in 1974 agreed to combine the administrations of the District's Teachers College and the Federal City College. In 1977, under President Jimmy Carter, plans were implemented to combine the schools to create the University of the District of Columbia (www.udc.edu).

UDC is the only land grant urban institution and is the only school in DC to offer reduced tuition and fees for DC residents. One of the school's central missions is to provide access to post-secondary education for DC residents. UDC charges $75.00 per credit hour for DC residents and $185 per credit hour for non-residents (http://www.udc.edu/academics/admission.htm).

These institutions have a rich history in the nation's capital. Each institution, either by founding mission or recent strategic planning, has a commitment to enrolling, educating and graduating an ethnically diverse student body. These efforts are reflected in each institution's online prospectus. What is not apparent, however, is their commitment to the richly ethnically diverse students who reside in the District. Based on these available perspectives, these institutions also do not provide information on the DC Tuition Assistance Program and, more importantly, how DC residents have or can in the future take advantage of the program to attend the DC colleges and universities.

The preceding perspectives offer available insight on DC colleges and universities student profiles, as well as federal and District approval and perceived success rate of the DCTAG program. They offer an excellent description of the role each plays in the District; however, they do not address strategies to make the public more aware of the program. Nor do they offer insight on how local schools participate in the DCTAG program, the impact the program may have on DC colleges and universities' general student enrollments, or the schools' ethnic diversity. This chapter explores DC residents' perceptions and level of awareness of the program and its impact on DC college and university attendance and ethnic diversity.

Data Analysis

Table 1 reveals that all 220 participants responded, and 49.1% were unaware of the DCTAG program. Of these respondents, 38.7% were aware of the programs and also knew it provided money for high school students to attend college. However, 4.5% thought that it provided access and opportunities, but not financial assistance, for students to attend college. Only 4.1% of the respondents were aware of the program because they personally received assistance from it, and 3.6% thought it provided money solely to students from low-income families to attend college.

Table 1: Frequencies for What Residents Know about the DC Tuition Assistance Program Awareness (N=220)

Response	N	%
Not Aware of Program	108	49.1
Gives Money to Attend School	85	38.7
Access and Opportunity	10	4.5
Recipient	9	4.1
Provides Money for Low-Income Families	8	3.6

Table 2 shows that 44.1% did not respond to question two; however, this can be explained by the large percentage of respondents, 49.1%, in question one who were unfamiliar with the program. Despite the high percentage of non-response, 24.5% of the 220 respondents learned about the DCTAG program through some form of media (newspapers, radio, print ads, posters, and the Internet). Of the 123 respondents, 14.1% learned about the program from friends, families and neighbors. However, 7.3% did not remember, 6.4% learned about it from school officials, and 3.6% learned about it from their own children who were preparing to attend college with the assistance from the DCTAG program.

Table 2: Frequencies for How did Residents Learn about the DC TAG Program (N=123)

Response	N	%
No Response	97	44.1
Media	54	24.5
Family, Friends and Neighbors	31	14.1

Don't Know	16	7.3
School Officials	14	6.4
Own Children	8	3.6

Table 3 reflects 204 respondents' perceptions on the DCTAG program increasing ethnic diversity at DC colleges and universities. Of these respondents, 28.1% said no, but 28% said they were unsure, and 24.4% said yes. However, 1.9% respondents said yes, if there is affordable access for students, 10.5% said no and offered a variety of reasons. Some of those reasons included student's desire to leave home and DC colleges and universities being too expensive, elite or competitive admission standards. Finally, 7.2% had no response to this question.

Tables 3 and 4 had similar responses, but the numbers of respondents were different. Of the 189 respondents in Table 4, 35.9% were unsure if the program would increase enrollment in DC colleges and universities, 19.9% respondents said yes, and 16.7% respondents said no, 31 14% did not respond to this question. However, 11.8% respondents said no with reasons. Those reasons included the perception that DC students may want to leave the District, the high cost, elitism and competitive admission standards would deter students from attending DC colleges and universities.

Table 3: Frequencies for Whether DCTAG Increases Ethnic Diversity at DC Colleges and Universities (N=204)

Response	N	%
No	61	28.1
Don't Know	62	28
Yes	54	24.4
No with Reasons	23	10.5
No Response	16	7.2
Yes, with affordable access	4	1.9

Table 4: Frequencies for Whether DCTAG Will Increase DC Colleges and Universities Enrollment (N=189)

Response	N	%
Don't Know	79	35.9
Yes	44	19.9
No	36	16.7
No Response	31	14.0
No with Reasons	26	11.8
Yes with Reasons	4	1.4

Conclusion and Recommendations

Based on the preceding results, there are differences between federal and District governments' perceptions of the DCTAG program and the DC residents' perceptions of it. Also, there is a difference in how the colleges and universities perceive student body ethnic diversity and enrollment, and the way the residents view student body ethnic diversity.

Of the residents who were aware of the program, more knew that it provided funding for students to attend college and a few knew the specific details of the program. Even fewer were recipients of the tuition assistance, and other respondents who were aware assumed that the aid was limited to students from low-income families living in the District. In addition, despite the noted success of DCTAG, the majority of the respondents were unaware of the program. Those respondents that were familiar with it knew that it provided financial assistance but were unaware of the program's details and the number of students assisted by the program since 1999. The high proportion of residents unaware of the program also explains the high level of non-responses on the second question which asked how they learned about the program.

Respondents that said yes with reason perceived the enrollment and ethnic diversity increase possible, only if families could still afford the tuition once the assistance was provided. However, it is important to note the three very significant reasons given for why the DCTAG would not increase diversity and enrollment in DC colleges and universities: (1) student's desire to leave their hometown to attend college would decrease the chances for increased ethnic diversity and enrollment, (2) the local schools' reputation of having extremely competitive admissions standards and high tuition cost would always be a barrier to increasing diversity and increase enrollment, and (3) residents' limited awareness of the program in turn limited the number of students applying for the assistance.

The unawareness and misperceptions surrounding this program provided perceptions which are varied and prompted the following recommendations and suggestions for future research which are paramount to the continued success of the DCTAG program, DC redevelopment goals, DC colleges and universities, and the DC high school students desiring to pursue higher education. The first recommendation is that federal and District officials should devote time and money to increase awareness, advertisement and understanding of the DCTAG program.

The second recommendation is to ensure that the colleges and universities referenced in this study try to develop more aggressive strategies to encourage enrollment form DC high school students, as well as make their participation in the DCTAG more visible to all residents of the District. This would increase enrollment as well as ethnic diversity. This recommendation supports the findings which indicated that many of the respondents perceived DC students' admission and attendance at local colleges and universities, with the exception of UDC, as unattainable. Due to the high cost and admission standards of these institutions, the DCTAG program alone would not be enough to increase diversity or increase general enrollment. These perceptions hold several implications which go beyond institutional admissions standards. Therefore, it is also recommended that further research is needed to understand DC high school students' preparedness, their rate of acceptance and matriculation to all DC colleges and universities.

It is equally important to examine the program's influence on students returning to DC to live upon graduation. Towards this end, it would be beneficial to conduct research to explore if the DC students attending colleges out of state influence the District's redevelopment plan, overtime, for the next generation of professionals in the District's economy.

In addition, we know, based on previous perspectives, that approximately 5,000 students received funding in 2006. But, how many more students are not inquiring or receiving funds due to lack of awareness or misperceptions about the program? Therefore, the third recommendation would be to investigate the demographic profile of awarded recipients, where they live in the District, ethnicity, gender, etc. to confirm the success rate and inclusiveness of this program. Without this knowledge we are unsure of the ability for this program to increase enrollment, in general, or ethnically.

As stated earlier, the DCTAG program was developed with District redevelopment goals in mind, by providing DC residents with access to in-state-tuition benefits from other states without leaving the District. This incentive appears to be beneficial to some residents. But how can we be sure that those residents who choose to stay are doing so only for the DCTAG benefit? As a result, there should be further research on how the DCTAG program affects DC families' decision to remain District residents. More importantly, is it enough to depend on current residents remaining for the District to continue its redevelopment plans? If not, it is recommended that strategies be developed to attract DC college graduates who were assisted by DCTAG to return to the District to work, live, intern or mentor younger DC residents.

Finally, it would be beneficial for the colleges and universities and the District to develop collective partnerships which provide more visible opportunities for DC residents to have better access to all schools in the District. Also, they should collectively develop goals that will help, not only serve the residents and students' higher education goals, to create better perceptions of the schools for the residents of the District.

5

National Education Association

+

Maryam Labeebah Muhammad

Introduction

For 149 years, the National Education Association (NEA) has been an integral part of American history, politics, and the educational system. The NEA was born out of a need for a national voice for teachers and public schools in Philadelphia, Pennsylvania on August 26, 1857 (NEA Gallery n.d.). Associations at the state level had already met this need, and their founders and leaders vigorously worked towards making a national association a reality. One hundred participants attended this historical occasion where 43 founding members signed a constitution and crafted a mission statement to promote education in the United States and to elevate the character and advance the interests of the teaching profession (Butler 1987).

Today, NEA boasts 2.7 million members, and the mission statement still mirrors those basic ideals, but takes them a step further by including "to fulfill the promise of a democratic society and to expand the rights and further the interest of educational employees; and advocate human, civil, and economic rights for all" (About NEA—Mission n.d.). In the early years, NEA activities were limited to yearly conventions, and membership was restricted to men, except for two women that attended the founding session (Butler 1987). Today, NEA membership is comprised of, but not limited to, NEA retired members, public school teachers, faculty members, counselors, librarians, nurses, school administrators, education support personnel such as secretaries, classroom aides, custodians, maintenance workers, bus drivers, food service personnel, nurses, school administrators, students preparing to become teachers, and others who hold teaching certificates (Join NEA n.d.). NEA's current budget of over $279 million and approximately 555 employees at the Washington, District of Columbia (DC) headquarter's office, and six regional offices are indicative of its political relevance and implications for educational policies and issues within Washington, DC (Fact Sheet—NEA n.d.).

Over the years, NEA's activities have evolved to include, but are not limited to, lobbying, advocacy for teachers' rights and benefits, endorsement of political candidates, supporting initiatives and legislation that advance quality teaching and education, and building alliances, partnerships, and collaborative working relationships with businesses and community stakeholders (Butler 1987). Other educational issues that are high on NEA's radar screen are accountability and testing, class size, school safety, charter schools, privatization, the No Child Left Behind Act, school quality, mathematics and science, teacher shortage, teacher quality, special education, student success, technology in schools, vouchers, and Wake-up Wal-Mart (NEA Education n.d.).

The objective of this chapter is to delineate the perceptions of DC residents regarding the NEA. The relevance and importance of this chapter is that the NEA affects political issues, which directly or indirectly impact the lives of all DC residents. The major questions investigated in this chapter are the following: Are you aware of the role that the NEA plays in DC education? What role does the NEA play in DC education? Does the NEA affect the educational policies in DC? These questions comprised the survey instrument for this chapter.

Review of Existing Perspectives

Since this is new research, there is a scarcity of available research regarding DC residents' perceptions of the NEA. However, the available literature discusses NEA in the role as a union and as a political power broker. Adam (1982) asserts that teachers' unions are political organizations. Unions speak for teachers; and like other unionized employees, teachers deserve to be heard and they deserve to be represented (Adam 1982). Unions provide policymakers at the local, state, and federal levels with expert knowledge regarding school operating conditions and concerns, thereby serving a vital role (Adam 1982). School organization, operation, practices, and polices are influenced by the teachers' union political activities (Marshall 2005). Unions work to advance the economic interests of their members, to pursue their own interests, and look for ways to improve the working conditions, salaries and benefits of the membership (Marshall 2005).

Lieberman (2002) contends that the NEA and the American Federation of Teachers (AFT) are the two largest teacher unions and they wield massive power over school employees and public school teachers. NEA and AFT have dominated the market for teacher representation services since the 1960s by maintaining control over representing teachers. NEA and AFT are against school choice, which translates into options such as charter schools, vouchers, and home schooling (Lieberman 2002).

From its inception until the 1950s, the NEA evolved from a men's club into the union era wherein union tactics and strategies were adopted to improve the wages, working conditions, and hours of work (McGray 2005). In 1972, NEA formed political action committees at the federal, state, and local levels to elect pro-education candidates to federal office (Stephens 1983-1984). The NEA has emerged to be one of the nation's largest labor unions with 13,200 chapters spread out across the country and recently they opted to let local chapters join the American Federation of Labor and Congress of Industrial Organizations (AFL-CIO) (Greenhouse 2006). Through NEA's coordinated nationwide lobbying efforts, the establishment and financing of a citizens committee, and prominent supporters in education, labor, civil rights, government, and business, Jimmy Carter's bid for presidency was successful; and the Department of Education was created (Stephens 1983-1984). In an address to the Economic Freedom Forum, Stefan Gleason (1999), Director of Development, National Right to Work Legal Defense Foundation, postulates that as the number of teachers paying union dues increases so does NEA's political clout. Gleason (1999) asserts that NEA's goal is political power and not meaningful education reform (p. 1).

As part of NEA's lobbying efforts at the national and state levels it has submitted letters to Congress requesting the rejection of the House Continuing Resolution 376, which would cut federal education, and amend the Resolution to add $7 billion for education and health programs (Letter to the House 2006). In the same letter, the NEA asked the House of Representatives not to include any reconciliation instructions that could affect student loans or other education programs and attached an addendum requesting funding for Pell Grants and the No Child Left Behind Program (Letter to the House 2006). Due to its political and monopolistic power, NEA has been able "to control the destiny of public schools and defeat reforms that limit its control over teacher certification, job security, and the working environment" (Closson n.d.). Parents should keep abreast of national issues and political trends to ensure that educational choices available to their children such as home schooling, vouchers, and charter schools continue to be available as a viable choice (Closson n.d.).

The NEA's political spending and activities have come under scrutiny by the U. S. Labor Department and the Internal Revenue Service because of complaints lodged by the Landmark Legal Foundation (Archibald, 2004). The controversy stems from the NEA supposedly giving away $65 million dollars last year to advocacy groups such as the Rainbow PUSH Coalition, The League of United Latin American Citizens, and the Gay and Lesbian Alliance Against Defamation Media Awards (McCluskey 2006). NEA responded to these assertions by indicating that most of the $65 million disbursements were grants given to NEA state affiliates (McCluskey 2006). McGray (2005) of the New York Times indicates that NEA contributed three million dollars to Democratic campaigns in 2004 and very little monies were given to Republicans. The NEA contends that political expenditures and spending were reported properly and they believe that investigations being conducted by the Internal Revenue Service and the Department of Labor will leave the association with a clean bill of health (Archibald 2004).

The limitations of these perspectives are that they focus on NEA from a historical and a global perspective. Additionally, available research does not include the voices of the DC parents, students, union members, teachers, concerned citizens, and/or other stakeholders. Therefore, capturing a complete picture of NEA's role and its affect and impact upon DC education and educational policies was challenging. Despite these limitations, recent literature suggests that NEA is indeed a powerful union and a consummate political power broker. The research findings presented in this chapter creates a body of knowledge that directly addresses the role NEA plays in DC education, what that role is, and whether the NEA affects educational policies in DC.

Data Analysis

A survey instrument comprising the three questions mentioned in the introduction section was developed to determine DC residents' perceptions of the NEA. A random telephone survey was conducted during the period of March through April 2006 with 219 DC residents. The data collected were inputted into the statistical package for the Social Sciences (SPSS) and the analysis comprised descriptive statistics: frequency scores and percentages.

Table 1 shows that out of 219 respondents, over 77 percent of them were unaware of the role that the NEA plays in DC education, 20.5 percent were aware of NEA's role, and 2.3 percent have very little knowledge of NEA's role. The responses to Question No. 1 also indicate that a large number of respondents is not aware of the role of the NEA plays in DC education and also a large number of them is not aware of the impact and influence NEA 's activities have on compelling DC educational issues and concerns.

Table 1: Are you aware of the role that the NEA plays in DC education? (N=219)

Response	N	%
Yes	45	20.5
No	169	77.2
Very little	5	2.3

Table 2 reveals that out of 219 respondents, over 66.7 percent did not respond to the question, 13.7 percent did not know what role NEA plays in DC education, and the remaining 19.6 percent offered some indications of the perceived role NEA plays in DC education. The responses indicate that the majority of the respondents did not respond to this question. It should be noted that when respondents answered no to Question No. 1, in most instances, they did not respond to Question No. 2. The themes raised most often by respondents were that NEA is a union, a lobbying group, an advocate for better education, and a trainer for teachers. Other themes raised were NEA's role is to set standards for schools, to conduct research, and to test the kids.

Table 2: What role does NEA play in DC education? (N=219)

Response	N	%
No response	146	66.7
Advocate for Better Education	7	3.2
Conduct research	2	0.9
Don't know	30	13.7
Governance of teachers, schools, and curriculum	1	0.5
Lobby group	7	3.2
Policy advisor to School Board	2	0.9
Provide funding for schools	1	0.5
Set standards for schools	3	1.4

Teachers' union	12	5.5
Test the kids	2	0.9
Train teachers	6	2.7

Table 3 indicates that out of 219 participants surveyed, 36.1 percent did not respond, 21.5 percent responded that they did not know, 17.8 percent responded yes, 16.4 percent answered maybe, and 8.2 percent answered no. The responses indicate that the majority of the respondents did not respond to this question. It should be noted that when respondents answered no to Question No. 1, in most instances, they did not respond to Question No. 3.

Table 3: Does the NEA affect the educational policies in DC? (N=219)

Response	N	%
No response	79	36.1
Don't know	47	21.5
Yes	39	17.8
Maybe	36	16.4
No	18	8.2

Conclusion and Recommendations

This study was conducted to determine DC residents' perceptions about the NEA by asking the following questions: Are you aware of the role that the NEA plays in DC education? What role does the NEA play in DC education? Does the NEA affect the educational policies in DC? The results indicate that over 77 percent of the research population was not aware of the role that the NEA plays in DC education, three percent had some knowledge of the role NEA plays in DC education, and 17.8 percent thinks the NEA affects educational policies in DC.

A consistent finding in the data analysis and the available perspectives section is that respondents and non-respondents are unaware of how NEA affects educational policies in DC. The available perspectives seem to suggest that parents should be more vigilant about legislation that is being introduced at the local and national levels to ensure that school choices currently available are not eliminated. This research is therefore important because it alerts individuals to the necessity of developing collaborative relationships to monitor ongoing dialogue and legislative processes to stay abreast of changing educational issues and reform. Also, knowing that a large number of DC residents are unaware of NEA's role in DC education as well as its affect on educational policies in DC provides an opportunity for proactive strategies to be developed and implemented.

The first recommendation is to conduct focus groups that would include teachers, parents, residents, community members, and students to identify their perceptions regarding NEA as well as to gather insights and recommendations about how best to keep them informed about NEA's role and activities. The second recommendation is to develop and administer a survey to teachers, parents, and students to rank the insights and recommendations raised in the focus group sessions. The third recommendation is to develop a communication strategy and timetable to disseminate information at specific time intervals via a newsletter, flyers, postcards, or E-mail to parents, teachers, faith-based institutions, and residents regarding NEA activities that have implications for the DC educational system. The fourth recommendation is to establish a liaison type position within each school to interact with the NEA to keep students, parents, and the administration apprised of NEA activities and issues of concern. The fifth recommendation is the collaborative sponsorship of theme schools and summer camp programs by NEA, the School Board, DC government, and the schools for students around public policy issue that impact the DC educational system. The sixth recommendation is to design and implement a political activities café for middle and high school students which will hold scheduled activities such as vignettes, role-plays, and brown bag sessions focused on public policy, social and political issues. Political activities would be open to parents and all school employees. The seventh recommendation is the creation of a student political action committee at each DC school. This committee would research current and proposed legislation that would impact DC schools, develop fact sheets, and hold discussion fora using the McLaughlin Group format. The eighth and last recommendation is to leverage Internet technologies and establish a Web site for each school, which would be updated as appropriate to educate concerned constituencies about NEA activities that directly or indirectly impact public education in the DC. These Web sites should also be hyperlinked to the School Board and the city government Web sites.

6

United States Congress

◆

Yiesha Thompson

Introduction

*District of Columbia Public Schools is a broken school system ...
racked by decades of neglect and mismanagement.*

—School Board Member Tommy Wells

*The D.C. Public Education System is broken. [It] is characterized by
competition rather than cooperation; by distrust, of new ideas and
Congress, rather than compromise; by self-interest, rather than the
interests of the school children.*

—Senate Report 104-144, 1996

The current condition of the District of Columbia's public school system
(DCPS) is devastating and heartrending. From dilapidated buildings,
inadequate school supplies, low teacher morale and substandard curricula,
public school students are being denied educational tools and academic
opportunities. Recognizing that the District of Columbia is not a state, the
United States Congress is charged with "ultimate plenary power" over the
District. Ultimate plenary power, according to the United States Constitution, emphasizes that Congress is not bound by the Tenth Amendment,
which states that, "Powers not delegated to the United States by the Constitution, nor prohibited by it to the States, are reserved to the States
respectively, or to the people" (US Constitution 1791). Therefore, Con-

gress has the "right to review and overrule locally created laws" which could positively impact and shape the District of Columbia.

Dating back to 1804, Thomas Jefferson was elected to the Board of Trustees for schools in the District of Columbia. Shortly thereafter, an act was passed to establish "permanent institutions" where children would be able to acquire a free education. While this act also allocated an additional $1,500 a year, African American children were unable to benefit monetarily (Hurlbut 1981). Lacking funding and resources, only two schools were able to launch and successfully operate. Subsequently, from 1804 to 1874, the evolution of the public school system in the District of Columbia began to disperse into four separate jurisdictions according to one's economic and social well-being. From Georgetown, Washington County and Washington City to the impoverished slums of African American territory, public education would only be advantageous for those who had a social and constitutional right to be treated as human beings (Hurlbut 1981).

In 1862, Congress recognized that it held the power of the purse and acted in accordance with the law to open a public school for Black children who resided in the District of Columbia. But, because segregation was prominent, Black schools operated under different superintendents and systems than their White counterparts (Hurlbut 1981). As time changed, so did the climate of the District of Columbia's school system and mentality of the Supreme Court and Congress. With the Court's decision in *Bolling v. Sharpe* (1954), desegregation soon became the mood in the District. Nevertheless, a century of inadequate supplies and inappropriate instruction had been placed on African American students, resulting in lower test scores, second-rate reading comprehension, and minimal math skills as compared to students in Caucasian schools. As a result, Congress instituted another bill hoping to alleviate some of the handicap and close the gaps in education and achievement. Although these changes took place over two centuries ago, today Congress is still trying to find the right mix to close the disparities in education and provide opportunities for all students.

Over the last decade, congressional members have fought on behalf of lower-income families concerned about the quality of education and safety of their children in DC public schools. While numerous initiatives have been voted down by Congress and vetoed by former President William J. Clinton, certain initiatives such as the District of Columbia School Reform Act of 1995 and the DC College Access Act of 1999 were passed and proved beneficial for underprivileged students attending public schools in the District of Columbia. To further assess DC residents perceptions of whether or not Congress had been influential in restructuring DCPS, a telephone survey was administered (by the principal investigator) to a random population of 223 residents, asking what role, if any, Congress played in DC public schools. The telephone survey also assessed whether or not respondents believed Congress should be more active in the DCPS system. After conducting the survey, the data collected were analyzed using the Statistical Package for the Social Sciences (SPSS) and descriptive statistics were used to compute the responses.

Review of Existing Perspectives

The District of Columbia Public School (DCPS) system currently consists of 167 schools, ranging from elementary to high school. Because these schools remain a "ward" of the United States Congress, four sub-committees have been established to help create effective change. The four sub-committees consist of (1) the DC Subcommittee, Senate Appropriations; (2) DC Oversight, Senate Government Affairs; (3) DC Oversight Subcommittee, House Appropriations; and (4) the DC Subcommittee, House Government Reform and Oversight. While all of these subcommittees have a profound effect on the District's daily management and funding allocations, the main problem that remains is that the members who serve on these subcommittees do not represent the District's residents or its interests. These members, with the exception of Eleanor Holmes Norton, are elected officials from outside states such as Ohio, Louisiana, Illinois, Virginia and Florida. Hence, it is understandable why previous initiatives to restructure DCPS have failed in the Senate and House.

Prior to the passage of the District of Columbia Reform Act (1995) and the DC College Access Act (1999), the only legislation that passed in regards to improving DCPS was the Even Start Family Literacy initiative (1988). In an effort to promote student achievement, this act sought to "break the intergenerational cycle of poverty of literacy in low-income and low-literate families" (Sivasubramaniam 2003: 2). Passed as an addendum to Title I of the Elementary and Secondary Education Act (ESEA) of 1965, the District of Columbia Reform Act sought to assist parents by providing them with "basic or secondary education and literacy programs," as well as "resources to effectively promote their children's educational development" (2003: 1). Although reauthorized in 1994, the DC Reform Act and DC College Act were needed to provide an "impetus to level the playing field and brighten the future for DC students" (CRS 2003: Article 3).

Seeing the lack of resources and unexplainable conditions of DCPS, Representative Tom Davis in the 107th Congress began demanding reform and co-sponsored the DC Parental School Choice Incentive Program (also known as H.R. 2556). In a 1999 *Washington Post* editorial, Davis asserted that "Relief needs to be provided [to end] the long standing challenges facing students in the District of Columbia public school system. Too many kids in our Nation's capital are not getting the education they need and fully deserve!" (NARPAC 2001: 12) Opponents to this bill argued that

> If the private schools employ exemplary academic practices, let's copy them—starting now. If the private schools want to pitch in, they can lend us their best and brightest teachers and administrators. If congressional leaders want to do their part, they should hold off on vouchers and permit public schools to implement the lessons they are already learning under the one year old federal No Child Left Behind law, a model of public school accountability. Let's use the archetypal strategies of the private schools *in* the public schools. Let's import the academic models, not export our children. We can copy their work; but private entities will never imitate our mission (DCPS 2005-2006: 3)

Other opposing scholars argued that legislation only passed because it was an omnibus bill—"a mammoth piece of legislation that crams all remaining bills into one, spending hundreds of billions of taxpayers' money in one fell swoop" (Lukas 2003: 1). Proponents of H.R. 2556 asserted that lower income families should not have to worry about the quality, safety and under-performance in District of Columbia public schools (Lukas 2003). The bill sought to offer parents with "trapped" children in DC public schools an alternative option. This federally funded voucher would provide lower-income families an opportunity to receive $7,500 for tuition, fees and transportation. Priority would be given to children who qualify for the free and reduced lunch program and listed those in Title I schools (Title I schools will be addressed in the latter portion of this chapter).

DCPS is rated last in quality public education, according to the National Assessment of Education Progress (NAEP 2002). According to *Reading 2000: Report Card,* DCPS children were reported as the "worse readers in the country" (NAEP 2002). Current statistics also indicate only six percent of fourth graders in the District tested proficient or higher in math, while the dropout rate for high school students is about 40 percent (CRS 2003: Article 3).

The Scholastic Aptitude Test indicated an average score of 702 for DC students, as compared to a national average of 896. Statistics also show that 20 percent of the DCPS students are classified as special education students, which is twice the national average for school districts (www.greatschools.net). As a result, the implementation of H.R. 2556 allowed these disadvantaged children and low-income families an opportunity to exercise the freedom of choice currently enjoyed by their effluent counterparts and congressional members.

Over the past decade, there have been numerous attempts by congressional leaders to pass legislation regarding low student performance in the District of Columbia. Earlier initiatives such as Amendment 90, H.R. 1350, SR 104-144 and DC Scholarship and Opportunity Act of 1997 are examples of blocked and vetoed legislation. One reason the effort to reform DCPS had failed is because there was no accountability. Congress does not hold principals and school boards accountable for mismanagement of resources and an unclear vision.

In the *Senate Report 109-106*, Congress directed DCPS to use funds to recruit and retain qualified principals and teachers to strengthen leadership and classroom instruction. During this period, five superintendents headed the DCPS system over a seven-year period. The superintendents were charged with drafting a proposal explaining how DCPS would use appropriate money and submit a report within 30 days (Senate Report 109-106 2006). Missing the deadline, Congress had to retract some of the funds allocated for the following academic year. Thus, it is Congress's job to step in and ensure that improvement and academic progress are being made.

Another problem is that presiding members who oversee the District of Columbia's school system represent other states which have needs different than those of DC constituents. Due to the fact that these members come from outside the DC area, one would wonder why these members would want to help transform the conditions of DCPS. Another question is the following: What are the benefits for these Congress members? According to Lukas, "members are understandably anxious to go home to their own families and districts, not stay and fight for a program that doesn't affect their constituents" (2003: 4).

With these questions lingering in the minds of the public, the National Heritage Foundation (2003) conducted two anonymous surveys of congressional members who practice school choice. Findings from the 2000 and 2003 surveys found that 46 percent of House Representatives send or have sent their children to private schools, as compared to 41 percent on the Senate side. These data showed 47 percent of Senate Finance Committee, 29 percent of the Congressional Black Caucus and 46 percent of Congressional Hispanic Caucus members exercised their private school choice (Kafer and Butcher 2003). These findings are significant because only 10 percent of American students in the United States attend private schools.

According to a study published in *Money Magazine*, students who attend adequate public schools outperform students in most private schools (October 1994). Susan Choy, in *Principal Magazine*, also argued that students' success is not based on their attending a private school, but rather based upon their abilities, attitudes and problems at the school

(Choy 1998). Subsequently, it is clear that members choose to send their children to private institutions based on choice, rather than the challenges and/or qualities the schools offer.

While the figures are alarming, they suggest that most elected officials prefer to send their children to private schools (Kafer and Butcher 2003). Members are more likely to exercise private school choice versus other Americans, so it unambiguous why members have failed to support previous legislation, which would allow parents in the District of Columbia to exercise this same right. These findings further portray how members of Congress view a situation when their children or grandchildren are not a part of the equation. Such statistics influenced House Government Reform Chairman Tom Davis to state that "Congress can no longer avoid its responsibility for the nation's capital under the Constitution" prior to proposing legislation (NARPAC 2001: 3).

In *Moms for School Choice* (2003), Carrie Lukas reported about a personal interview she conducted with Tracy, a mother in the District of Columbia. Her article focused on a mother who withdrew her children from public school and still continues to fight for change on behalf of her neighbors. While Tracy fully understood that Congress determines whether or not DC parents have an option for their children, she also believed that "mothers deserve to control where their children go to school" (Lukas 2003: 1). Like Tracy, many parents no longer want to settle by sending their children to DC public schools, but many of them cannot afford to do otherwise due to factors such as personal income and increasing unemployment rates—especially for single family homes. Therefore, the passage of the DC Parental School Choice Incentive Program (H.R. 2556) was not only instrumental for DCPS, but also for 57 percent of the DC parents (Kafer and Butcher 2003).

The DC Parental School Choice Initiative Act

To begin the improvement of DCPS, Congress passed legislation aimed at helping low-income children attending schools in the District of Columbia. Known as H.R. 2556, the DC Parental School Choice Initiative Act of 2003 was the first bill of its kind in the District. Secretary Paige, Former US Department of Education, reported H.R. 2556 as "a major victory for kids trapped in bad schools" (2003). As a result of the bill, parents would have the option of sending their children to private, charter or parochial schools. A better education is the objective of the bill, and only 1,500 students out of 65,000 would be given this opportunity on an annual basis (Sanchez 2004). This is because a criterion for the plan indicates that children must come from families of four or more, earning $36,000 or less annually.

Qualified applicants of H.R. 2556 would be placed into a lottery system, and 1,500 students would be awarded a scholarship of $7,500 for tuition, fees and transportation. Although an overwhelming number of the parents were in favor of the bill, there were still some major concerns. First, some parents feared that the federal government would play a major role in the schools their students attended. Senator Edward Kennedy and Ms. Sandra Feldman (then President of the American Federation of Teachers) contended that "private schools currently screen their applicants and are reluctant to take kids who are too far behind academically to do well. Religious schools, Catholic schools in particular, on the other hand, have embraced the plan" (Sanchez 2004: 2). Although parents would have the opportunity to place their children in better schools, the schools they chose may not accept their children. Hence, disparity will continue to increase, rather than decrease. Subsequently, H.R. 2556 would benefit less than one percent of currently enrolled DCPS students (Hsu and Blum 2004).

Data Analysis

After the principal investigator conducted telephone surveys of randomly selected DC residents from February to April 2006, respondents' perceptions were analyzed. To provide accurate information regarding the attitudes of DC residents regarding the public school system, the survey focused on three questions: (1) Are you aware that the US Congress plays a role in DC public schools? (2) What role does the US Congress play in

DC schools? (3) Do you believe that the US Congress should be more involved in DC public schools?

It was founded that 66.8 percent of the 223 respondents were aware that Congress played a role in DCPS. However, of this population, 40 percent were unable to indicate the details of the role that Congress played in the DCPS system. Contrarily, 30 percent of respondents knew that Congress controlled and oversaw DC public schools budget and 17 percent of respondents knew that Congress represented the District of Columbia as a state. In regards to whether or not Congress should become more involved in DCPS, the respondents were split with 43 percent in favor of more involvement and 44 percent against increased involvement. The remaining 11 percent did not know, but believed that children and additional resources in DC public schools should be the focal point rather than "party politics" (see Tables 1-3).

The most interesting aspect of the data was the attitude respondents had regarding Congress's role in DCPS to ascertain adequate teachers. Some 2.2 percent of the respondents believed that Congress should mandate the accountability of teachers and staff before issuing funds to a school; but in the DCPS school system, this is not the case. Teachers are interviewed and hired through a DCPS process in which Congress does not interfere.

Additionally, question three accentuated whether or not residents believed that Congress should be more involved in DCPS. Respondents were split almost 50/50. However, an alarming 11.2 percent expressed that members of Congress should be more involved, "as long as they look out for our kids and ascertain adequate funding and resources" (survey respondent, March 2006). After further examination, these residents also maintained that Congress should be more involved with the selection process of qualified teachers, staff and personnel. One respondent contended that

> Teachers and staff are not compassionate about the work they do. They don't even call home to let parents know when something disruptive has occurred at school or in the classroom. How are parents suppose to parent when they are not on the same accord as teachers and principals

[administrative staff]? This is the problem parents' face in the District of Columbia (April 2006).

These same respondents also agreed that Congress should be more involved in DCPS meetings to alleviate and/or resolve mismanagement issues and offer guidance, so that intended action can occur swiftly and expeditiously.

Of the respondents who knew the role of Congress in the DCPS system, they also believed that it was Congress's job to ensure accountability from principals and teachers. This was important because while Congress votes to distribute funding to DC public schools, it does not take into account the schools standardized test scores, safety issues, or teacher vigilance, as most parents indicated during the survey.

Table 1: Are you aware that the US Congress plays a role in DC public schools? (N=223)

Response	N	%
Yes	149	66.8
No	74	33.2

Table 2: What role does the US Congress play in DC school? (N=223)

Response	N	%
Oversees the budget	73	32.7
Oversees the DC public school system	15	6.7
Represents DC as a state	39	17.5
Don't know	91	40.8
Miscellaneous	5	2.2

Table 3: Do you believe the US Congress should be more involved in DC public schools? (N=223)

Response	N	%
Yes	98	43.9
No	100	44.8
Don't Know	25	11.2

In addition, a study conducted by the *Center for Education Reform* (2005) found that more than 70 percent of the schools in the District of Columbia were identified as Title 1 schools, which emphasizes that they were in need of improvement for 2005-2006 (2005). The study also found that 90 percent of southeast DC schools were listed as Title 1, versus 71 percent in northeast DC and 32 percent in northwest DC.

According to NAEP (2006), Title 1 seeks to ensure that schools meet adequate performance and annual progress for three consecutive years or more. The title also looks to exhibit fair, equal and significant opportunities in obtaining a better education and advanced proficiency on challenging state academic achievement standards. When children attend schools that fall under Title 1 status, the parents are given an option to either use a school transfer or supplemental service. School transfers are awarded to parents so that they can transfer their children to schools *not* identified as dangerous or "in need of improvement." Supplemental services, which include tutoring or extra academic aid, are also available to these parents (Center for Education Reform 2006).

In a report prepared for a March 2000 conference on vouchers, researchers Patrick Wolf, William Howell and Paul Peterson analyzed H.R. 2556. Since its implementation, in 1999, they reported the following findings:

1. Ninety-five percent of program participants are African American (a pure reflection of DC population);

2. Fifty-three percent of recipients who were offered a scholarship accepted, while 47 percent declined;

3. Students who applied and accepted the scholarship (grades 2-5) outperformed their public school peers by seven percent in math and three national points in reading[1];

4. Whereas 15 percent of public school parents gave their children's schools an "A" grade, 46 percent of private school parents did as well;

5. Sixty percent of private school parents are happy with safety issues, compared to 26 of public school parents;

6. Private schools are more likely to have after-school programs and additional resources like tutoring services or classes for the "young and gifted";

7. Fifty-six percent of private school parents are satisfied with school curriculum, versus 70 of public school parents;

8. Fifty-five percent of public school parents continuously report serious issues such as destruction of student property, fighting, cheating, ample absences and tardiness in relation to 25 percent of private school parents (Wolf, Howell and Peterson 2000).

Although Wolf, Howell, and Peterson's evaluation offered insight on how children and parents coped with the transition from public school to private or parochial schools, the evaluation also highlighted three potential problems of H.R. 2556. First, H.R. 2556 fails to specify whether or not funds would be earmarked. Second, parents who were schooled in DCPS may want to send their children out of the District to receive a better education. Third, the bill's short-term plan bequeaths numerous children,

---

1. Numbers are significantly different for children in middle and high schools because children tend to adjust easier at younger ages. Studies show, "older students, in contrast to students in lower grades, reported less enthusiasm for their new school; older children were also more likely to be suspended, and scored lower on the reading test than their public-school peers" (Wolf, Howell and Peterson 2000).

because younger recipients, who accept the scholarship, will not be able to use it due to overcrowded classrooms.

Conclusion and Recommendations

Due to years of repugnant conditions in the District of Columbia public school system, members of Congress excitedly voted on H.R. 2556, also known as the DC Parental Choice Act, in an attempt to remedy educational gaps. While this short-term effort sought to reform DC public schools, studies show both positive and negative effects. Ideally, the plan allows parents of children in the District of Columbia to have a choice of where they want to send their children. On the other hand, only a small number of children are able to benefit from the option. Therefore, it is suggested that Congress should offer additional incentives to teachers, principals and superintendents or utilize option B (presented in Appendix 1), so that more children can benefit annually.

One flaw with the School Choice Bill is that it fails to indicate whether or not funds will be earmarked and allocated annually to those students who qualify for the program. When the bill passed in the House, Congress approved 13 million for the program. However, there are currently 65,000 students enrolled in DCPS (Davis 2003). Subsequently, only 1,500 students would be warranted an opportunity to excel academically, while the remaining 99 percent are forced to remain at schools with dire conditions.

A possible recommendation to alleviate this problem would be to incorporate Fred Hiatt's option. According to Max Pappas (2004), Hiatt contends that school choice is necessary because parents "feel trapped between sending their children to dangerous and dismal schools and not sending them at all" (*Washington Post* February 28, 2004). As a result, Hiatt believes that Congress should design a system in which the parent of each pupil is given a $10,000 check and allows principals to promote and sell their schools. Not only would this rack transparency, it would also ensure accountability. Additionally, it seems that students would benefit because high morale teachers would be attracted to these schools and monetary gain to the schools could drastically improve the schools' conditions.

A second flaw with the School Choice Bill is that many parents who were educated in DCPS now opt to send their children to private or parochial schools. Although most private schools have additional resources that are not available at most DC public schools, children may need additional help with instruction and homework. As a result, parents must be able to assist children more often. However, if parents did not receive an adequate education while attending DCPS, they may not be able to comprehend the work given to their children. Therefore, two plausible suggestions are brought forth to aid parents of children in the DCPS system. First, parents should be highly encouraged to join the Parent Teacher Association (PTA) in order to support children's transition into private or parochial institutions. Second, various strategies should be implemented to provide parents with explicit learning tasks and activities in which they can engage to effectively assist with their child's academic growth. Also, as a result of attending PTA meetings, parents would have better rapport with teachers and principals, which will benefit their children's success in the long run.

A third problem is that teachers may migrate to schools with better performing students and higher pay. As a result, children in underperforming schools may be exposed to uncompassionate and/or under-prepared teachers, which can result in low student enthusiasm and test scores. In order to retain good teachers at low performing schools, superintendents should provide incentives to teachers. By allowing teachers a chance to increase students' test scores and excite them to learn, the curriculum and/or superintendents should provide quarterly or annual merit bonuses for the schools or individual teachers. By doing so, teachers will have a desire to ensure that children are being stimulated and reach their full academic potential. In turn, children will reap the benefits. Also, schools like Simon Elementary in southeast, Banneker High School in Northwest, and School without Walls in Northeast should be tracked and studied to see how change positively shaped student grades and test scores.

A fourth problem is that H.R. 2556 is a short-term plan. According to Wolf, Howell and Peterson (2000), during the 2001 academic year, middle and high school students no longer were able to accept scholarships due to overcrowded classrooms. Currently, DCPS is known for its overcrowded classes; however, private and parochial schools pride themselves on a 13:1 student-teacher ratio (Wolf, Howell and Peterson 2000). There is a huge mismatch between the number of high school spaces available and the number of students seeking options. In the fall semester of 2005, 1,029 students were awarded "opportunity" scholarships; and as of spring 2006, there were still 40 to 60 high school students looking for schools due to overcrowded classes (Wolf, Howell and Peterson 2000). In two years, there will be 606 students receiving scholarships in junior high; but by the time they reach high school, there will be no room for them to use their scholarships (2000). If no action is taken, nearly 75 percent of students holding scholarships to attend high school will be unable to use them because of limited capacity.

A suitable recommendation to this problem is to propose and implement a budget of $10,000 per parent, as described by Fred Hiatt (*Washington Post* 2004). Pappas outlines Hiatt's budget proposal to distribute a $10,000 check to each low-income parent of a DCPS child. With this option, nearly 90 percent of the children in DCPS could acquire further educational development or acquire quality education, as opposed to only helping 1,500 students with H.R. 2556 annually (see Appendix 1).

Indeed change needs to occur within the DCPS system, and the passage of H.R. 2556 has shed light on the poignant situation and provided opportunities to lower-income families. According to the survey results, 57 percent of the residents in the District of Columbia were excited about the passing of H.R. 2556. However, many residents voiced negative concerns about Congress acquiring additional involvement. Forty-Four percent argued against additional Congress involvement, because Congress failed to mandate accountability. Contrarily, 11.2 percent of residents expressed that involvement would suffice as long as Congress "issued additional funding to public schools" (survey respondent 2006). Thus, it is imperative for Congress to review DCPS. Children in the DC public school system are constantly being denied a better future and it is evident that this can no longer be tolerated. Subsequently, while this bill looks to address the issue of reform in DCPS, the ultimate goal should be to alleviate educational gaps and provide DC children with lifelong opportunities.

Appendix 1

H.R. 2556: Current Plan	Option B: Hiatt's Plan
13 Million for Voucher	10,000 per parent
$7,500 per pupil at	Principal is charged with selling the school(s)
1,500 students per year	
	65,000 pupils enrolled
= 11,250,000. VS.	10,000 * 65,000
/ 65,000 pupils enrolled	= 650,000,000
= 0.057	
Hence, less than 1 percent of DCPS students are being helped each year.	Hence, funds are distributed equally and more than 90 percent of DCPS students are able to acquire quality education.

The difference between the current plan and Option B is the number of children who will benefit from assistance annually. Although the current earmarked allotment is set at 13 million for DCPS, less then 1 percent of District of Columbia's disadvantaged children will be able to gain and solidify quality education. Contrarily, Option B looks to decrease the division by ameliorating Congressional funds and increasing alternatives plans for parents to utilize, so that their children will have better opportunities.

7

The White House

◆

Stan Warren

Introduction

This chapter seeks to determine the perceptions of residents of Washington, DC on the "No Child Left Behind" (NCLB) program initiated by the Bush Administration some years ago. At its inception, the president and his education department heralded the program as a means to assist students to improve their tests scores.

However, the feedback from a myriad of DC parents and others who have interest in educational issues have negated the euphoria of the administration. After the "No Child Left Behind" program was touted as an initiative to facilitate students in improving their grades, it was not followed up with appropriate financial backing and infrastructure support to maintain the project. There has been perennial clamor by school superintendents who have complained about the depletion of their budgets in funding the program, and they have yet to be reimbursed by the federal government.

Several states have distanced their governments from the program stating that it is too bureaucratic in its operation and is taking personnel and time away from educational programs that have been functioning well prior to being coerced by the Bush Administration. Their actions have resulted in threats by the administration to withhold funds to states that remove themselves from the program. However, a plethora of states have made good on their threats, and the federal government has withdrawn its intended draconian response because of the groundswell in opposition to its policy.

The Bush Administration argues that countries like Cyprus, South Africa and other territories that do not possess the technological or financial capacity as the US have moved ahead of the leader of the free world. "No Child Left Behind," according to the president, is an initiative to get the country on the right track. He further said that the government has been injecting billions of dollars in education without follow-up evaluation to assess the results of the financial injection.

Review of Existing Perspectives

The following are differing perspectives by individuals who have expressed their views on the impact of the NCLB since its inception in 2002. Several comments expressed scathing opinions on the program's effectiveness where it has proved impotent in augmenting primary through secondary educational landscape.

The program's meandering journey has developed numerous loopholes after several amendments to its original intentions. Schools tend to find a myriad of ways to circumvent the tenets of the NCLB. Schools knowingly refuse to count accurately and omit minorities in relation to their test scores to appear favorable at the end of the assessment period. This action has affected almost two million children who are kept out of the tabulation process (Bass, Zieglar et al. 2006).

Furthermore, NCLB allows states to exclude test scores from racial categories with varying numbers in the testing groups. Oklahoma does not count 52 or fewer members in its testing population, while Maryland and Washington have five and 18 exemptions respectively. Areas where English is a second language and inner-city locations where Blacks have problems in mastering the language have been experiencing disenfranchisement (Freudenberg 2006).

Based on the NCLB Act, schools are assessed in three categories that include learning disabled, economically disadvantaged, or learning English as a second language. Local officials have complained that the NCLB is ineffective and unfair because schools can be penalized if they fail to meet standards set by the program in one of the three categories (Bromley 2006).

The NCLB is far from being a bulwark in strengthening the nation's educational program; flaws in the law have been undercutting its original purpose and have worsened the educational landscape of the United States. The future of children's lives are at stake, and the Department of Education needs to make positive improvements in its NCLB program with appropriate measurement in reference to effectiveness of schools (AFT 2006).

The NCLB Act of 2002 has augmented the English awareness of Limited English Proficiency (LEP) children. It helps parents to monitor their offsprings progress in school by the children being tested in reading and language arts after three years of school attendance in the United States. The program also allows guardians with children enlisted in LEP to monitor and make sure that teachers are fluent in written and oral English and that they have good communication skills (Boehner 2002).

States are constantly faced with obstacles entrenched in the program that prevent local officials from instituting innovative and flexible approaches to the federal act. States need to be fully funded if the tenets of NCLB are to be carried out; states should request Government Accountability Review to confirm the economic strain on the local education system. Additionally, the government should remove the one-size fits all approach in states' requirements; students should not be grouped into one category, because they learn at different rates (NCSL 2005).

As part of the NCLB program, states are mandated to provide tutoring for children who have difficulties in maintaining their grades. However, the identified students are not receiving the needed lessons because several school districts continue to have problems in finding learning centers that are willing to take on the assignments. The potential tutors espouse that the school districts are rural and do not have enough students to be cost-effective to promote their business. Therefore, several million dollars are left unspent, which could have otherwise been put to good use in the school system (Goldstein 2006).

Not much	28	12.8
Not sure	2	0.9
It is a Presidential program	56	25.7
It provides better education	29	13.3
It is a strict program	1	0.5
Teachers and students get left behind	1	0.5
I know something	14	6.4

Question number two did not receive its full compliment of respondents; 18 of the interviewees did not express any opinion when asked. Forty-five respondents had no knowledge of the program, and 100 persons said that No Child Left Behind would not improve the performance of DC schools.

Table 2: Is the No Child Left Behind Program improving the performance of DC schools? (N=218)

Response	N	%
Don't know	45	20.6
It is ineffective	1	0.5
No	100	45.9
Not sure	31	14.2
Slightly	1	0.5
Yes	22	10.1
No response	18	8.3

There were two hundred responses to question three. There were 50 don't know responses to this question, but the highest number recorded was the "no's" that showed a total of 60 respondents.

Based on the survey results, respondents clearly rejected the No Child Left Behind program initiated by the Bush Administration. The positive responses derived from the three questions were marginal when compared to the total respondents contacted. Question one had 14 "yes" responses and 29 said the program provides better education for children.

The second question received had a total of 63 affirmative responses where of the interviewees, 22 persons said "yes," 31 were not sure, and one "slightly sure." Question three featured 58 "no" responses and one maybe.

Clearly, the Bush Administration had not done its due diligence before implementing the program. Persons perceive the program as an exercise in test taking without regard to the retention level of students. In the "ridiculous" responses, the interviewees felt that the children were being treated as mechanical beings that are being scurried through the educational system based on Bush's tests. Those who are unable to master the tests are subsequently left behind, although these children are intelligent.

Table 3: Were DC schools better off before the No Child Left Behind Program? (N=218)

Response	N	%
Don't know	50	22.9
No	60	27.5
Not really	1	0.5
Not sure	28	12.8
For political reasons	1	0.5
Same	26	11.9
Schools, no, teachers, yes	2	0.9
Yes	32	14.7
No response	16	7.3

Programs that are geared to help students improve their grades should be dependent on computerized test taking. Students should be allowed to do written exams where their weaknesses can be ascertained easily and remedied through counseling. Additionally, students learn at different rates, and it is best to facilitate the educational abilities of the children rather than creating robots.

The program's insatiable appetite to gain "good" results has propelled the administration to exclude certain ethnic individuals to arrive at overall passing rates for states. This approach has pressured local educational entities to become involved in actions that are not beneficial to students in order to obtain passing grades and receive the promised input.

Conclusion and Recommendations

Based on the myriad of displeasures with the NCLB program, clearly, the administration needs to revert to the drawing board to reassess both the nature and the long-term effect of this education initiative. Apparently, the program is being pushed through various regions of the nation without setting up test areas to see its effect on the identified children.

The displeasures with NCLB are not only with the professionals within the system but, most important, they also come from parents who feel that their children are being short-changed and being passed over to achieve a targeted quota. Parental frustrations have permeated the media, and the numerous articles in local and national publications evidence these feelings.

The inability to locate tuition for students who are in need of this important facet of the program speaks volume to the shortsightedness of NCLB. The United States is a large country in term of both length and breath; a country of this magnitude will definitely have rural areas in need of special attention. The program should have set up a system to address areas that do not have the wherewithal of the big city, which can generate the volume of students necessary to create business incentives for tutoring organizations.

The way forward to improve NCLB's performance is to work with parents and professionals who play an integral part in the educational process. This can be achieved by conducting nationwide town hall meetings to hear the feelings of individuals who have lived the ineffective results of the program; officials can then undertake measures to address NCLB's shortcomings. Everyone wants the best education for the nation and her/his children; but to be effective, the 'top-down' approach is not the best way forward. Professionals, parents and students also have a part to play in decision-making process. The administration needs to include the 'bottom-up' approach to take into considerations all concerns in its policy.

The Administration needs to revise its formulae in reference to the starting points for the yearly progress in the program. Additionally, improved monitoring services should be implemented to ensure that the Supplemental Education Services, a part of NCLB, provide the tutoring functions. Further, latitude should be given to states to formulate their methods of qualification for teachers who work in charter and public schools (Smith 2006).

Data Analysis

This survey was conducted to elicit a panoramic response from the capital city to garner feelings about the program. A three-item questionnaire was constructed, and respondents were randomly contacted by telephone. Two hundred and eighteen persons responded to the survey.

In reference to question one, which is stated below, there were 16 different responses. They range from "a joke" to "a ridiculous program." The comment with the highest response number is "presidential program." Twenty-nine respondents stated that the program provides better education for the children. One respondent said that the program is strict. All subjects responded to question one.

Table 1: What do you know about the No Child Left Behind Program? (N=218)

Response	N	%
It is a joke	2	0.9
Don't know	13	6.0
Educational program	13	6.0
It has failed	23	10.6
It is a mess	1	0.5
It is a ridiculous program	8	3.7
It is set up to help rich in school	1	0.5
It sucks	1	0.5

8

Private School Education

✦

Vernese Edghill

Introduction

The initial intent of this chapter was to discuss private school success by
exploring graduation rates of private schools' students by race, ethnicity
and gender. However, the published SAT mean scores guide this analysis
of private school success in Washington, DC from 1998 to 2005. This
chapter defines and explains the general purpose of private school education nationally and locally, and the various types of private schools which
exist. More importantly, this chapter brings to light differences in the
types of private schools in Washington, DC and how these differences are
reflected in high school student performance.

The District of Columbia is an urban center with vast resources and educational opportunities. It is also a city with several different private school
opportunities for school age children from Pre-K to 12th Grade. Private
school education is different from public school education. Private schools
have the ability to choose the type of children and families to admit into their
institutions. Likewise, families and children have the opportunity to choose
the type of private school environment they would like.

Nationally, there are several different types of private schools. According to Alt and Peter (2002), there are Catholic, nonsectarian, and other
religious schools. The other religious schools include, but are not limited
to, Baptist, Episcopal, and Methodist. Non-sectarian schools, generally,
would include Montessori and independent schools, which do not have a

religious affiliation. Montessori and independent schools, however, often times have autonomous boards and academic curricula with unique and diverse school missions. Each of these three types of private schools have professional education organizations, national and local governing boards which monitor policies, funding, ethical standards, teaching practices and academic standards.

Private school education is primarily funded through tuition payments, private sources, foundations, annual giving, private donors and alumni contributions (Alt and Peter 2002). Unlike public and some charter schools, private schools are owned and governed by independent boards, generally religious organizations, and independent boards of trustees made up of parents and community leaders.

Most religious schools, especially within the Catholic school system, are generally governed by a local church and the national or international church affiliation. For example, the local church and the Roman Catholic Church govern Catholic schools, but autonomous boards govern independent schools, and most are also affiliated with the National Association of Independent Schools (NAIS).

According to the United States Department of Education's NCES Schools and Staffing Survey 1999-2000, nationally, 30% of the private schools are Catholic, 22% are non-sectarian, 49% are made up of other religious private schools. Approximately 39.9% of all private schools are located in urban areas (Alt and Peter 2002).

Each private school offers either elementary and/or secondary grade levels with each school's organizational resources, staffing, missions and goals autonomously determined. In addition, each school also offers different types of learning environments. Some schools are day schools, boarding, single sex, or cater to special needs populations.

Private schools in Washington, DC can be compared to private schools nationally. In 2004, *The Washingtonian Magazine* published a comprehensive list of all private schools in Washington, DC, which includes 57 coeducational, five single sex, two day schools, one boarding school for boys, two day schools for girls, and three schools for student populations with special needs. Of the 57 coeducational schools in the District of Columbia, 24 were Roman Catholic.

Private schools are typically sustained through enrollment and tuition. In Washington, DC, the costs of tuition for private schools vary and range between $3,000 for Pre-K annually to $10,000-$23,000 for Kindergarten through 8th and 12th Grade. Typically, Catholic schools' tuition average $7,000 for Catholic students and $7,200 for non-Catholic students per year. Generally, the average cost per child is approximately $2,000 to $3,000 (*The Washingtonian* 2004).

What makes private schools more attractive educational options is their administrations and boards' ability to create the type of school communities, and the sizes of the individual classes. Many of these schools tend to offer smaller class sizes, and there are smaller total enrollments which average from 27 to 100 students per grade level.

Private schools in Washington, DC are not new; and despite the array of schools, there are little written about them. This chapter provides a more in depth study of private schools, high school student success rates by type of private school—Religious Affiliated or Independent, and addresses critical questions which can assist schools, parents and children make more informed decisions when choosing private school education.

Review of Existing Perspectives

According to Preston (1940), prior to the 1800s, there were no schools for Blacks in the District of Columbia, but there were vocational and informal education Blacks were determined to receive in the District. Today, there is a plethora of opportunities for Blacks to be educated. These opportunities have tremendous value for the children, but at times financially and socially unaffordable prices for many. To better serve all populations exploring educational options for their children, it is important to understand the history, social and cultural mission and the academic rigor of private schools. The issues put forth in this chapter begin to broaden the understanding of the politics of private school education for all families.

Historically, private schools have been noted as being prestigious educational institutions. Catholic, other religious schools or non-sectarian schools, like independent schools, have been noted for providing academically rigorous curricula for all students who apply and are accepted. The related research and perspectives available attempt to explain and/or justify private school education's history, purpose, mission, objectives and publicized academic student performance. All of the research and perspectives on private school education has been approached with a variety of different themes, theoretical and methodological approaches. These varying perspectives suggest different outcomes for different children; they also choose different indicators to measure these outcomes. Some of these indicators include changing enrollment trends, increased tuition, competitive application and selection processes, recruitment and retention of diverse students and faculty, race, class, socio-economic status, and income.

The perspectives examined in this chapter provide insight into the governing organizations of private schools and advice for parents in well-known local and national magazines in Washington, DC and predictors of student success in private high schools. These perspectives are not exhaustive, but they serve as an example of the type of information currently available on private schools in general, and in Washington, DC in particular.

Private School Governing Organizations

Parents, alumni, and school administrators have written these perspectives. Some of these perspectives were written with parents as the target audience in order to provide advice and assistance on how to navigate a private school's admissions process.

The National Association of Independent Schools (NAIS) is a voluntary membership non-profit organization serving over 1,000 schools. It serves as an advocate of schools throughout the United States and aboard, over 45,000 students and faculty and administrators, and over 9,000 administrators. NAIS publishes a magazine called *Independent School* whose purpose is to make visible the mission and purpose of the organization. In 2002, the NAIS board adopted an Independent School Advocacy Initiative and published four statements that purposefully exposes the benefits of private schools. They are: (1) providing excellence and difference in thousands of communities; (2) modeling different routes to high-quality education; (3) being locally focused; and (4) teaching respect, tolerance and democracy (*Independent School* 2002).

On an annual basis, NAIS also publishes demographic and geographic statistics on the population profiles of independent schools by state/region. It also has published several articles based on personal accounts and school administrator testimonies on the high level of student success after graduating from independent schools. These briefs provide the organization an opportunity to highlight the positive rate of success students who attend independent schools experience. Many of these accounts utilize the students' rate of acceptance into Ivy League and other elite liberal arts colleges and universities in the United States. NAIS also uses these data to promote the benefits of private school education and the rigorous independent-thinking and liberal arts driven curricula unique to independent schools (*Independent School* 2004).

The Association of Independent Schools in the Greater Washington, DC area (AISGW) is a non–profit corporation which provides standards and sound educational practices to the independent schools in Washington, DC. This organization offers programs, retreats, and workshops for teachers, administrators and staff. A board of local heads of independent schools governs AISGW, just like NAIS. AISGW also seeks to work collaboratively with other parochial and public schools locally, regionally and nationally.

Public versus Private School Education

The following paragraphs review research on private school related issues reflected in different disciplines and political interests. The focus is on how private schools are impacted by race, class, socio-economic status, attainment, vouchers, diverse populations, and education accessibility. Although the works examine different indicators related to private school education, the one underlying issue addressed by all of the literature is the true benefits of private versus private schools.

"Public School Quality, Private Schools, and Race" (1999), written by Wrinkle, Stewart and Polinard, studied the use of two theories which might explain the correlation between public school performance and private school enrollment. The first of the two theories used is "market reform theory" which suggests that the decline in public school performance heavily influences private school enrollment. The second theory is Smith and Miewr's suggestion that the choice of a private school is driven by a family's need for religious instruction and a racially segregated environment. In order to analyze both theories, they used a dataset of 73 Texas counties from 1991 to1995. Wrinkle, Stewart and Polinard found that the market reform theory could not be supported; however, there was some relationship between private school enrollment and families' need for their children to have religious instruction

In "Do Private Schools Force Public Schools to Compete" (1996), Arum addressed the unending debate on public versus private schooling. Arum argued that much of the debate often negates the relationship between public school students' performances and each state's variation of size in the private school sector. He posited that organization efficiency can account for better public school performance, but it is dependent upon a state's size of its private schools system. The larger a state's private schools system, the better public school performance becomes because of more and improved resources. Large private school systems would then create a need for the public schools to improve their offerings and resources to compete with other more resourceful educational systems.

Several articles offer research and data from achievement test scores and elite college acceptances as determinants of the benefits of private school education. However, according to Coleman, Hoffer and Kilgore (1982), high achievements of students in Catholic and non-sectarian schools are equally comparable to public school students when school polices and the students' behavior in accordance with the school's policy are similar to the behavior of students attending Catholic or non-sectarian schools.

School Choice and Parental Choice

Vouchers are a governmental educational benefit created to improve public school systems and resources and to give parents and students in poor school systems the opportunity to choose better schools in the community. Vouchers can be used in better public, charter, or private school systems. There are several works on voucher systems arguing both pro and con. More importantly, there are varying perspectives about the use and misuse of vouchers for students already enrolled in private schools.

School choice is a benefit to a private school education; however, school choice in conjunction with universal voucher systems precipitates much debate. According to Friel, in his article, "Public or Private School? It's your Choice" (2005), states that the theoretical uses of voucher versus the actual distribution of vouchers need to be further explored and determined. He discussed the advantage of vouchers, how public school advocates perceive the effects of the voucher system, and the problems with assessing voucher systems. Without further investigation, he argued that it is impossible to consider the voucher system a success.

Although there is a large body of literature on private schools and voucher policies and related studies, there are equally as many articles on more personal experiences and perspectives to help parents and policy makers understand the realities, challenges, competitiveness, parents' rights and privileges associated with choosing private or public schools. For example, in an article entitled "Parental Choice" (2004), Vaishali Honawar argued that officials who often promote policies for good public school systems choose private school education for their own children. Jack Jennings (2004), director of the Center for Education Policy, also believed that in addition to hired governmental officials, few presidential and government officials, who in fact support public education, do not choose public school education for their own children. Honawar (2004) also interviewed Margaret Spellings, domestic-policy adviser, and Krista Kafer, an education policy analyst at the Heritage Foundation. Both suggested that before determining a particular private school, it was essential to consider the child's needs first. All private schools are not the best fit. They themselves, as parents, have made similar choices for their children that resulted in having children in both public and private schools.

Private Schools, Race and Socio-economic Status

Some literature used the 1970's Census to determine which variables influenced sending children to private schools. According to Long and Toma, in "The Determinants of Private School Attendance" (1988), family income, religion and the supply of schools available in a particular region are key variables. Although they are very important variables, they also note that in the 1970s, when variables such as race and income were added, decisions were narrowed.

So an appropriate question that should be asked is the following: Who can afford, without the use of a voucher system, to send their children to private schools? To answer this question, there have been several studies that explore socio-economic status, educational attainment and private school choice. These variables are important to explore, since many of the private schools, with the exception of Catholic schools, were generally financially unattainable elite institutions. Due to the changing economic status of Blacks in the 1970s and 1980s, however, these affluent schools now have more middle class and working class children enrolled. The increased enrollment, nonetheless, is not enough to assist students of color in some elite private schools. In order to navigate these systems, Slaughter and Johnson, in *Visible Now: Blacks in Private Schools* (1988), wrote on a range of topics to assist parents familiarize themselves with the private, affluent school environments. They offered perspectives from Black parents on their experiences in private schools, an analysis of Black parental involvement in these communities, and the historical trends and patterns associated with the recruitment and support of Black students in private schools. They also offered historical insight on Blacks' support for urban Catholic schools, quality education for Blacks, and policy and parental strategies to increase academic success and greater access to private schools (Slaughter and Johnson 1988).

One article which promotes Catholic School education, especially for Blacks, is "Getting the Job Done Well: African American Student and Catholic Schools" by Vernon Polite (1992). In this article, Polite gave an historical analysis of Catholism and Catholic Schools since the beginning of the colonial era. He also provided documentation which illustrates the relationship between the earlier African Caribbean settlers in the colonies in the 1500s. He posited that this relationship developed as a result of the Code Noir that supported a more liberal treatment of free mulattos and French and Spanish slaves. As a result of these territorial laws, African American girls were educated in Ursuline Academy in New Orleans in 1727 (McDermott and Hunt 1991). In addition to the earlier African settlers, one of the oldest Catholic schools founded for African American children is St. Augustine in Washington, DC, established since 1858. Following the establishment of St. Augustine, 76 other Catholic schools opened to serve African American children. Polite also argued that there was an increase of African American students in Catholic schools from 170,000 to 220,000 in 1991; but due to White student enrollment decreasing and the numbers of other minority students increasing, the African American population in these schools was constant at 9% (Polite 1992). He attributed African American interest in Catholic school education as being historically traditional as well as the evidence of effective teaching models for African American Students.

The existing perspectives reviewed in this study address children's educational needs, parental choice, academic student performance, social, cultural and socio-economic issues related to private schools. However, it is important to note that family school choices, regardless of governmental and state policy initiatives, are fundamentally based on a family's socio-economic status and available quality educational opportunities. Although many of these influences determine school choice, these issues may not be considered when schools determine admission policies and measures for student performance in the District of Columbia. Overall, the perspectives suggest that students of all races experience great success in private schools, especially when comparing educational benefits and resources to public schools.

Data Analysis

The data analyzed in this chapter are mean SAT scores of male and female students in Religious Affiliated and Independent Schools in Washington, DC. These mean scores are used to determine if there are differences in

SAT student performances between Religious Affiliated and Independent Schools in Washington, DC. The use of three statistical procedures was to measure and understand SAT performances for these two types of schools. The univariate descriptive statistics (Table 1) explain the overall means of Verbal and Math scores for both Religious and Independent Schools. The bivariate statistics provided in a correlation matrix (Table 2) determine the relationship between the variables. To understand and interpret if the differences in means were significant a t-Test was used. However, to explain possible growth of mean SAT scores over time, a multivariate time series (Table 3) was employed.

Data Collection

A secondary analysis was used and data were collected and analyzed from The College Board's 1998-2005 *College Bound-Seniors State Profile Report District of Columbia*. The data used were the mean SAT scores for Religious Affiliated and Independent Schools for males and females in Washington, DC from 1998 to 2005. The mean, according to The College Board, is the arithmetic average of the SAT scores, and the scaled score is the scores converted from the actual raw scores of correctly answered questions minus a portion of the incorrect answers (The College Board 2005). The state reports are broken down into nine sections: (1) Academic Recorded, (2) Course-Taking Patterns, (3) Background Information, (4) College Plans, (5) Score Distribution SAT Reasoning Test, (6) Score Distribution SAT Subject Tests, (7) High School Information (8) Colleges and Universities, and (9) Scholarship Programs. These data are aggregated and, more specifically, they were derived from the High School Information section in the Type of High School category of the state profile reports from 1998 to 2005.

The Sample

The data for this study are aggregated data originally collected from the College Board of high school seniors who had taken the SAT Reasoning Test. This test was formerly known as the SAT I Reasoning Test and serves as an assessment of a student's ability to reason using the skills and knowledge acquired from the educational classes taken while in high school. Students filled out an optional Student Descriptive Questionnaire when they registered to take the SAT exam. This questionnaire was self-administered by the student and is used to interpret the scores by individual and groups of students who took the exam through March of the year the report was written (The College Board 2005).

Figure 1 represents the percentage of male and female students from both Religious Affiliated and Independent Schools in Washington, DC each year. Males range from 56% to 61 %, and females range from 39% to 42 % for Religious Affiliated schools. In Independent Schools, male students range from 49% to 53 % and female students range from 47% to 50%.

Schools

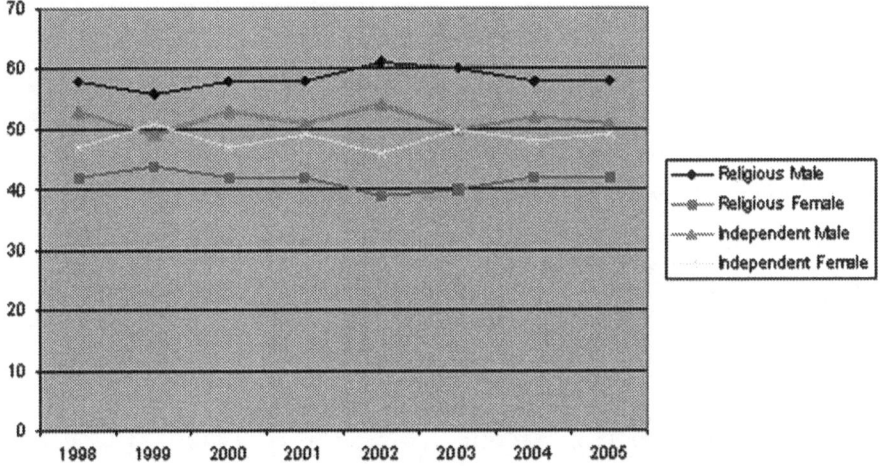

Figure 1: 1998 to 2005 Washington, DC in Private

Students in this study were only counted one time; so if the student took the SAT twice in one year; his/her latest and most recent scores are reported in the College Board State Report for each year. Data in this report are summarized and aggregated for the annual report. The state profile reports aggregated SAT score results of students in Washington,

DC by race, ethnicity and gender; however, the College Board does not report race, ethnicity and gender SAT mean scores by type of high school. Therefore, this study is limited to the percentage of male and female students reported in the Type of High School section.

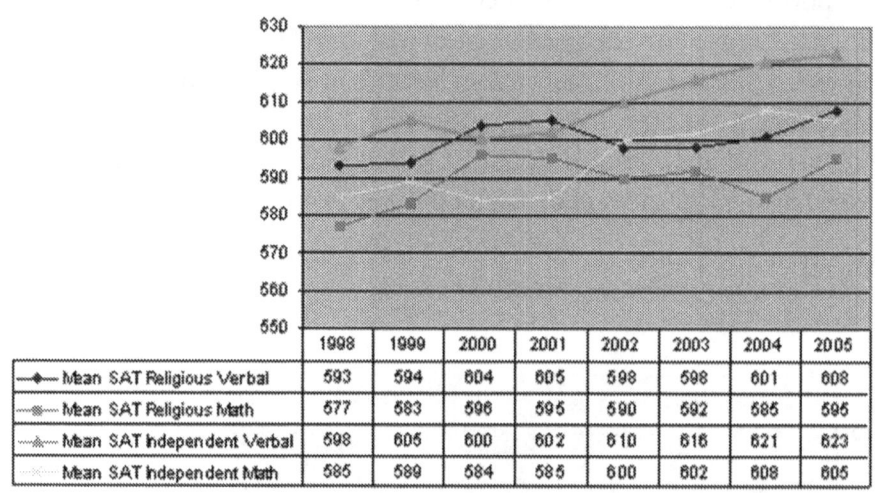

	1998	1999	2000	2001	2002	2003	2004	2005
Mean SAT Religious Verbal	593	594	604	605	598	598	601	608
Mean SAT Religious Math	577	583	596	595	590	592	585	595
Mean SAT Independent Verbal	598	605	600	602	610	616	621	623
Mean SAT Independent Math	585	589	584	585	600	602	608	605

Figure 2: 1998–2005 The Washington, DC College-Bound Seniors Average Verbal and Math SAT Scores

Figure 2 reflects the combined average mean Verbal and Math SAT scores for male and female students in Religious and Independent Schools between 1998 and 2005. The table also shows that in 1998, the Religious Affiliated and Independent School male and female mean SAT Verbal scores were 593 for Religious Affiliated and 598 for Independent Schools. However, it also suggests that over time, the average Verbal Score for both types of schools have improved, with SAT Verbal scores of 608 for Religious Affiliated and 623 for Independent Schools in 2005. Figure 2 also shows the same type of improvement in 1998 for Religious Affiliated and Independent Schools for males and females, as the mean SAT Math Scores were 577 for Religious Affiliated and 585 for Independent Schools. Over time, this Figure also shows the average Math Score for both types of schools improved with SAT Math Scores of 595 for Religious Affiliated and 605 for Independent Schools in 2005.

Results

The results in this section will help one to understand the differences in high school performances for male and female students in Washington, DC Religious Affiliated and Independent Schools. Table 1 shows that Independent Schools had the highest overall Verbal and Math SAT mean scores from 1998 to 2005 (Verbal 609.38 and Math 594.75).

Table 1: Univariate Statistics

	Comparison of Means	Standard Deviation
Religious Verbal	600.13	5.330
Independent Verbal	609.38	9.680
Religious Math	589.13	6.833
Independent Math	594.75	9.996

Table 2: Correlation Matrix

	Religious Verbal	Independent Verbal
Religious Math	.839** .009*	.235** .576
Independent Math	.218** .604*	.965** .000*

*p < .01 *(99 % Confidence Level)*

**Pearson-r/Sig. Level (2-Tailed)*

Table 3: Paired T-Test for Religious Affiliated and Independent School Math and Verbal SAT Scores

Paired Samples Test	T	Sig. Level
Religious Verbal* Independent Verbal	-2.875	.024*
Religious Math* Independent Math	-1.388	.208
Independent Verbal* Independent Math	15.817	.0001*
Religious Verbal* Religious Math	8.315	.0001*

*p < .05 (95 % Confidence Level)

The correlation matrix in Table 2 determines if the co-relationships between the variables are significant. The findings are that there are statistically significant co-relationships between Religious Math and Verbal mean scores (.009) and the same is true for Independent School Verbal and Math mean scores (.0001).

A paired sample t-Test was used to determine if there was a statistically significant difference in the Verbal and Math mean scores for Religious Affiliated and Independent Schools. When Religious Verbal and Independent Verbal Mean scores were paired, it showed that the difference in the mean growth of scores was negative and statistically significant (Table 3). This reveals that when one school's scores are going up, the other scores are declining. Conversely, the difference in growth for Religious Math scores and Independent math scores was also negative, but not statistically insignificant.

The paired sample t-Test also was used to determine that differences in mean score growth between Religious Verbal and Religious Math were positive and statistically significant. The same was true for Independent Verbal and Independent Math scores (Table 3).

Table 4: 1998–2005 Time Series for Overall Growth of Religious and Independent School Mean SAT Math and Verbal Scores

Variables	Autocorrelations	Standard Error	Sig. Level
Religious Verbal	*-.274*	*.158*	*.097*
Religious Math	*.043*	*.158*	*.886*
Independent Verbal	*-.293*	*.158*	*.017*
Independent Math	*-.269*	*.158*	*.010*

*p < .05 *(95 % Confidence Level)*

The fourth test employed was the time series (Table 4). This procedure was used to assess possible observed patterns of change in the mean of Verbal and Math scores between1998 and 2005 for both types of schools. Time series was employed to explain the improved SAT scores by more accurately identifying how Independents School students have shown marked improvements in mean SAT Verbal (.017) and Math scores (.010) at a 95% confidence level from 1998 to 2005.

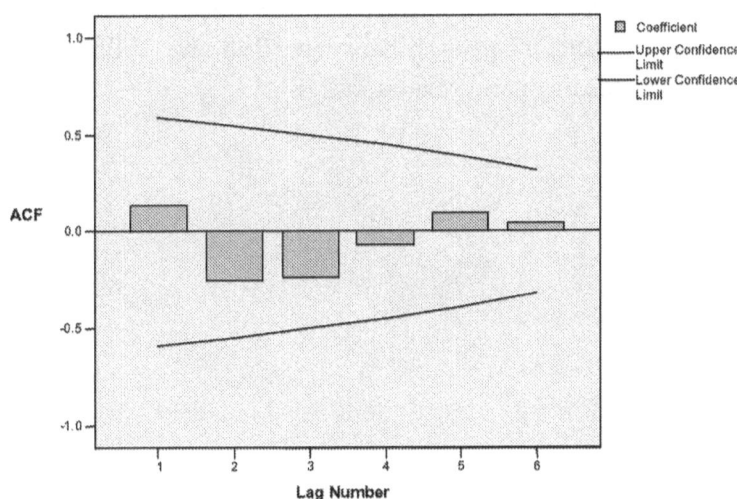

Figure 3: Change in Religious Affiliated Math

IndMath

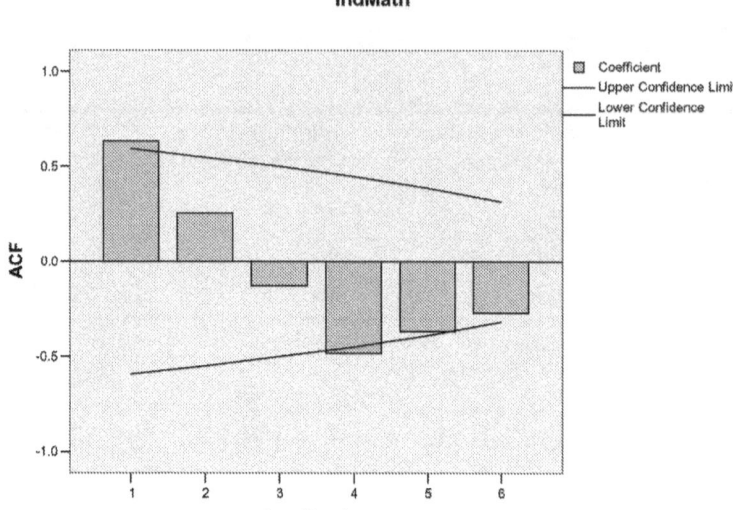

Figure 4: Change in Independent Math

Figures 3, 4, 5 and 6 also reveal the individual characteristics of the growth from both Religious Affiliated and Independent Schools' Math and Verbal means scores. It is evident that the mean Verbal and Math scores from 1998 to 2005 fluctuated more in Religious Affiliated Schools than in Independent Schools. Independent School scores had a positive and statistically significant growth between 1998 and 2005, which is evident in all of the findings and related tables.

RelVerb

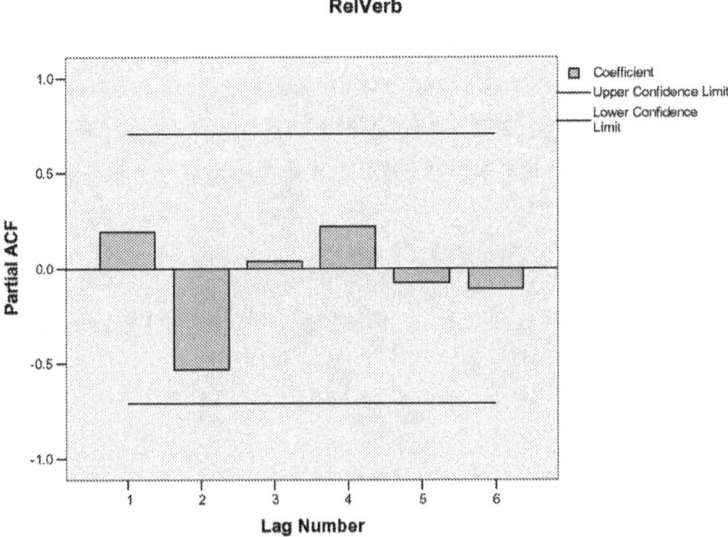

Figure 5: Change in Religious Affiliated Verbal

IndVerb

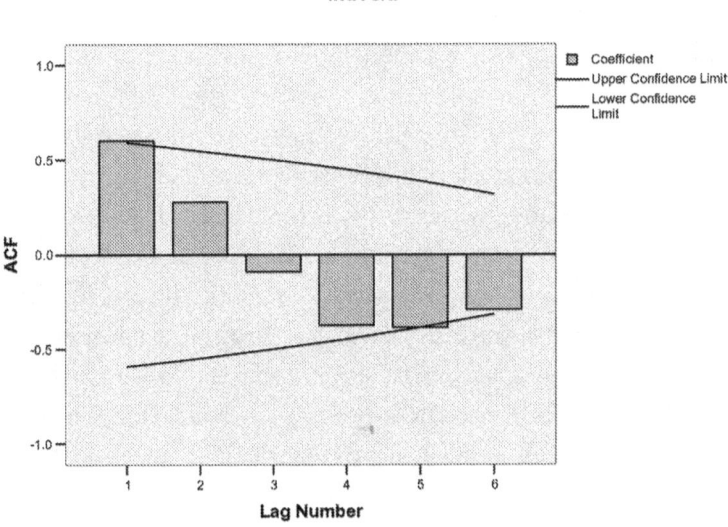

Figure 6: Change in Independent Verbal

Based on this analysis, it is obvious that even though over time both Religious Affiliated and Independent Schools have shown some improvements in SAT student performances, Independent Schools showed more significant growth and positive change in SAT test performances than Religious Affiliated Schools. This would suggest that if parents used SAT performance alone to determine a child's success in a school, Independent Schools would be the ideal schools for students.

Conclusion

Over the years, studies have indicated that standardized testing is culturally and racially biased, especially in the Scholastic Aptitude Test (SAT). Despite longstanding biases embedded in the SAT and others, these tests and related scores are used for most colleges and universities as a partial gatekeeper for college admissions processes for high school students. It is because of this age-old process a parent's secondary school choice is made based on how well a school will assist in his/her child's academic preparedness; prepared enough to be well-rounded, obtain the best SAT test performance in order to be in admitted into a "prestigious" college or university. Although SAT scores are a major determinant for college admission, it is not enough to rely solely on standardized tests to determine student success and school fit.

Based on the findings in this study, Independent Schools are the best environment for optimal student SAT performance. If parents with college bound seniors were made aware of this information, it would probably be in the student's best interest to attend an Independent School. However, Independent Schools, as stated earlier, are generally small elite tuition funded schools that require families to go through a competitive admissions process. This process limits students from lower socio-economic households the accessibility to these prestigious educational opportunities. As noted earlier, Catholic schools have historically been more accessible to diverse racial and socio-economic groups, more so than Independent Schools.

Consequently, there are several questions and concerns that would need to be addressed, if SAT scores remain a major part of college admission, and the best SAT student performers come from Independent Schools. Do private schools and college admission pools accurately reflect the nation's household and students' race, class and gender diversity? This question is difficult to answer because of the limited amount of data available on race, class and gender diversity in all types of private secondary schools nationally, and especially in the nation's capital. Therefore, a recommendation is put forth for educational officials, nationally, to begin to collect and analyze data on private school graduation rates and college matriculation, similar to available data on public school graduating seniors by race, class and gender.

Is it equitable for colleges and universities to continue to use the SAT as a major influence for college admission? Given the cultural and racial biases that exist in standardized testing and the limited number of students that can attend private schools, policy should be introduced to develop standardized tests which are more racially and culturally competent. Until these changes can be made, colleges and universities should not use SAT scores as a major determinant for college success and academic excellence.

More importantly, educational policies should also provide equitable school resources and academic preparedness, nationally, for all students, regardless of public or private school attendance. All students, regardless of public and private school attendance, should also be exposed to the same level of academic preparedness. This would help to ensure improved standardized test performance, regardless of the type of secondary school a student attends. It will also allow for better recruitment and retention of students, regardless of race, class and gender.

9

The State of the Public Schools

✦

Ronald C. Clark Jr.

Introduction

The meager performance of Washington, DC's public school children, pre-kindergarten through grade 12, has been one of the most historical, controversial and divisive public policy issues inside the capital region's beltway. As a result, the District's public education system has lived under intense scrutiny in the public eye by congressional politicos, educators, interest groups, and think tanks alike. Granted, there are many variables that have contributed to poor student academic achievement such as the inept decision-making in the Office of the District of Columbia Public School (DCPS) and the DC Board of Education (DCBE), underfunding, lack of resources, untrained teachers, teacher scarcity, and the elimination of specialized education programs. The concern over the District's children, however, has not solely been based on flaws and failure. Contention over student academic achievement in the District is largely entrenched in accountability, ranging from parental responsibility to negligence by the United States Congress. Although there are logical explanations that offer different perspectives, rationales and dynamics, proponents and opponents alike cannot provide a coherent, amenable solution to the lackluster performance of the District's youth. Thus, various aspects that affect student academic achievement in the District are explored in their entirety.

Public schools in the nation's capital have consistently ranked dead last among the nation's public schools systems in virtually every measure of performance, even though DC's per-pupil spending ratio has been among the highest in the country (Balko 2002). Accordingly, the DC State Education Agency indicates that 37 percent of the District's residents read at the third grade level or below (Lartigue 2002). Based on this account, it is easy to presume that the DCBE and DCPS have mismanaged essential supplemental resources and taxpayer money that has produced a considerable number of illiterate adults while vacating the educational needs of the District's children. Yet, neither the DCBE nor the DCPS or the legislature should absorb the brunt of responsibility for the systemic dysfunction that has resulted in poor academic achievement. The lack of parental involvement has had an astounding impact on student academic performance as well. The District's dropout rate is estimated at 40 percent (Lartigue 2002). In addition to the high dropout rate, the majority of the District's youth perform well below the national average on standardized tests in mathematics, reading, writing, and science. Perhaps that is why members of Congress felt the need to federally fund school vouchers for a proportion of minority children from low-income households in the District as a remedy to the bleak condition of DCPS. Yet, in contrast, DC children using privately funded vouchers have not demonstrated strong academic improvement (Norton 2003). Furthermore, challengers propose that DC's school voucher program is a legal vehicle in an incremental effort to privatize education rooted in political ideology and religiosity.

Nevertheless, despite the gross mismanagement and unconcerned mind-set of many, minority District parents of the capital's children have been systematically conditioned against learning. Consistent with other public school districts in urban America and contrast to suburbia, most of the District's youth are poor minorities who are forced to learn amid dilapidated buildings, an air of violence, lack of textbooks and materials, high student-to-teacher ratios, diluted curricula, and frustrated and uncaring educators. Hence, under these conditions in which basic needs are not met, it is hard to expect many students to read, write, and do math and science at high levels (Declaration of Education 2005). In essence, many DC students are unable to succeed because the system and faulty leadership do not prepare them to succeed (Lartigue 2003).

A proper analysis of student academic achievement among the District's youth cannot be conducted without reference to the impact of DCPS's unique governing structure. From a historical perspective, the District has had as many as four school systems: Whites-only, Georgetown, Washington County, and Blacks-only (Levy 2004). Likewise, the District once possessed an equal number of school boards before they were fused into one entity by Congress. Additionally, until 1974, local officials appointed by the United States President provided the funding to DCPS, while the school board, appointed by district court judges, ran the school system (Levy 2004). Presently, the District's mayor, City Council, DCBE, and superintendent all take part and contribute to the function of DCPS to varying degrees. Since DCPS's existence, the United States Congress has possessed the power to trump and dictate all budgetary decisions while exercising other vehicles of influence.

Since DCPS's ratification by Congress and operation under multiple systems of governance, the concerns and criticisms about the bureaucracy, influencing external forces, and subsequent consequences have persistently remained similar (Levy 2004). Granted, methods for improvement for student academic achievement have been debated by education officials and the legislature for quite some time. Yet, those in power have historically ignored and failed to improve conditions through inactivity or decisions that have produced the same deficient results. This is likely due to unclear lines of authority, unmotivated leaders, the bureaucratic process, and political manipulation. Collectively, these pertinent factors have all contributed to the poor academic achievement of the District's youth, and this has consistently been the norm for decades.

An accurate assessment of DC's public education system reveals a sentiment of unaccountability. For years, the District's leadership and stakeholders alike have focused on inputs rather than high standards of productivity without reaching positive results. Hence, in a call to reform America's deteriorating educational system, the No Child Left Behind (NCLB) was enacted under the pretext of alleviating educational disparity, mandating that schools, educators, and students alike meet stringent performance standards. Although NCLB has proven itself to be faulty in many respects, it overwhelmingly addresses the problematic issue of accountability and uniform standards for academic performance. Additionally, this legislation provides concerned parents an active voice and remedy in their children's education.

Given that there are numerous dynamics that directly and indirectly impact student academic achievement, it is reasonable to suggest that if it were not for the implementation of NCLB, the problems associated with poor academic performance would have likely persisted. Likewise, since the District's public education system has failed to remove itself from deterioration, it is comprehensible to believe why some constituents and bureaucrats prefer charter schools and voucher systems over public education, even though these avenues perpetuate a separate and unequal education, as it is sometimes argued. Nonetheless, the core of this chapter concentrates on the ills of poor academic achievement of the District's youth from 1996 to present, the impact of NCLB, and the likelihood for improvement. Specifically, this analysis addresses the following questions: What are the pertinent factors that have contributed to poor academic achievement in the District's public schools? Has the impact of NCLB helped repair student performance? Are school vouchers and charter schools actually necessary for improving the overall performance of the District's youth or are they politically motivated?

Review of Existing Perspectives

In the intense debate over student academic achievement in the District's public schools, many government officials, policy analysts, and concerned parents alike have expressed their disdain for poor student performance in the nation's capital. Some presume that voucher programs to private schools and charter schools are effective avenues to remedy poor academic achievement. Yet, others reckon that increased funding and resources to DCPS is the foundation for improving academic progress among the District's youth. However, despite the various strategies for educational reform in the District, it is universally acknowledged inside the capital region that the failure of the DCPS' stewardship is not a new phenomenon

(Lartigue 2003), and the concern of improving academic achievement remains consistent.

Poor academic achievement in the District's public school system reveals that abysmal leadership and the mismanagement or scarce funding and resources by the DCBE and school superintendents have resulted in a severely damaged and dilapidated school system. Thus, in 1995, the United States Congress passed and President Bill Clinton signed a law creating the District of Columbia Financial Responsibility and Management Board (also known as the Control Board) that effectively stripped the DCBE of power for approximately four years after characterizing the DCPS as being "dysfunctional" in its 1996 report, *Children in Crisis: A Report on the Failure of the D.C. Public Schools* (Lartigue 2002). In this study, the Control Board judiciously accentuated the failure of the District's public education system, defective leadership and lack of accountability, and alternative methods for progress and advancement.

In *Children in Crisis*, the Control Board asserted that the heart of the school system's problem is the pale leadership from the DCBE and Superintendent of Schools. As such, both have abdicated their responsibilities to the city and the children in their failure to provide a quality education in a safe environment (Children in Crisis 1996). Given that the DCBE and the Superintendent are primarily liable for student academic achievement, this report found both negligent and reckless in defining clear academic standards, budgetary oversight, administrative control, procurement, staffing, facilities management and, most significantly, the failure to strategically plan. In one particular mishap, the National Science Foundation rescinded a $13.5 million mathematics and science grant due to the District's failure to adequately plan and implement a math and science program (Children in Crisis 1996). In addition, this investigation revealed substantial shortcomings such as inequitable and weak standardized test scores, high drop-out rates, systemic problems with violent behavior, criminal activity and safety, persistent fire code violations and leaky roofs, delinquent textbooks for instruction, and 32% of classroom teachers that did not have required teacher certifications (Children in Crisis 1996). In sum, this examination charged that the DCBE and Superintendent were mutually responsible for contributing factors that prohibited progress and improvement in student academic performance.

In difference to deficient leadership and mismanagement, some argued that inadequate funding has been a principal cause for systemic dysfunction in DC's public schools, indirectly affecting student academic achievement. Peggy Cooper Cafritz, President of the DCBE, insisted that the lack of resources and financial investment has been the fundamental challenge in improving student academic performance. Given that annual budgets have been continuously reduced by the US Congress in concert with the underfunding of NCLB, essential programs and classroom services were eliminated (Cafritz 2003). Likewise, it has been intensely contended that school vouchers subtract from vital public education funding in the District. With $14 million under current appropriation levels, and diverted and allocated to the DC Opportunity Scholarship Program (DCOSP) through the Washington Scholarship Fund based on the DC School Choice Incentive Act of 2003 (as outlined in the Consolidated Appropriations Act of 2004), significant improvements that affect student academic achievement is subject to neglect in subsequent years.

Similarly, Joyce Ladner provided a distinct aspect of how funding variations between local school districts throughout the country and the nation's capital obliquely affect academic performance in her testimony before the United States Senate. Given that the District does not possess taxing authority or other reliable sources of revenue, the DCPS competes with other vital government programs for scarce tax dollars (Ladner 1998). In essence, unlike most local school districts, the District, to a large extent, cannot rest on property taxes for educational revenue. Likewise, Mayor Anthony Williams cited the inequitable and illogical nature of the District's fulfillment of county, city, and state functions with a severely limited tax base as a reliable funding source for public education (Williams 2003).

Moreover, in a contrasting posture that detracts from poor leadership, mismanagement and underfunding, competition, or the lack thereof in recent years, have been regarded as the basis and decree for pitiable academic performance of the District's youth. Staunch advocates of the

DCOSP maintained that if more money were the solution to poor academic achievement, then we would have solved the problems of public schooling in the District a long time ago (Hickok 2003). Similarly, proponents of school vouchers suspected that the leadership and management of DCPS have been beyond repair for decades. Thus, many politicians, schools officials, educators, and concerned parents alike considered the viability of school vouchers essential to educational reform in the District.

The premise of proponents' argument in favor of the DCOSP inferred that student academic achievement will not improve unless parents are awarded the freedom to obtain the best education possible for their children (Boehner 2003). In effect, champions contended that parental influence provides tangible leverage in holding school officials and educators directly accountable for student academic achievement. Given that families typically flee districts where schools under-perform and flock to localities where they succeed (Davis 2003), advocates vowed that competition between DC public school system and private schools correlates to betterment in academic performance. Subsequently, patrons of educational reform in the District presumed that competition ultimately improves the overall academic climate so that all schools are forced to improve (Boehner 2003).

Likewise, in a separate, yet parallel, endorsement of the DCOSP, supporters persisted that the District's public education system is merely a failed monopoly, in which a competitive climate incrementally depresses student academic achievement. In essence, without the DCOSP, proponents asserted that a monopolistic educational bureaucracy and framework prevent innovation and dull academic performance (Archibald 2004). Although documented research conducted in other urban cities suggested otherwise, empirical research performed in the nation's capital regarding privately funded vouchers for low income minority students demonstrated that there is a lack of overall achievement between public and private education (Ladd 2003). Furthermore, it has been aggressively argued that the lack of competition denies the District's dominant minority schoolchildren the moral and civil right to a fair and equitable education enjoyed by their Caucasian counterparts. From this perspective, patrons of the

DCOSP contended that those who qualify for school vouchers were given the opportunity to escape the deplorable conditions of the District's public education system. Yet, realistically, competition between public schools and private schools in the District spurred by the DCOSP is only speculative at best, because private schools select their students, whereas public schools must accept every child (Coalition for Accountable 2003). It has been effectively argued that private schools overlook students with special education requirements, students with limited English proficiency, behavior problems, and low levels of academic achievement (Toyer 2003).

Collectively, yet distinct, shoddy leadership and mismanagement, low budgets and resources, and a monopolistic culture are equally contributing factors in the District's barren academic performance. Given that *Children in Crisis* proposed that for each additional year that students stay in DCPS, the less likely they are to succeed (Children in Crisis 1996), lends credence to the deduction that sole accountability for lackluster performance of the DC's schoolchildren remains with the DCBE and subsequent Superintendents. However, since DCBE members previously and consistently rated former Superintendents above average and excellent on performance evaluations, resulting in higher salaries, the DCBE undeniably failed in its responsibility to hold Superintendents accountable for the state of the District's public schools. Therefore, it is easy to criticize and condemn the DCBE and Superintendents because they are legally answerable to student academic performance. Yet, from a broader perspective, the City Council, the District's Mayor, and the United States Congress are unvaryingly responsible in their failure to exercise power and political influence to remove incompetent school officials and board members.

Similarly, District parents should bear some responsibility for their children's academic performance. Yet, how much parental accountability should be expected when an estimated 37% of the District's adults are functionally illiterate. Moreover, given that the University of the District of Columbia reported that nearly 85% of its students who came from DCPS needed remedial classes (Balko 2002) exposed the link between poverty and low academic achievement. Thus, it has been ascertained that parental responsibility should be held to a minimum, because the historical social conditions affecting academic achievement and active involvement emphatically left parents without a choice. Hence, the educational bureaucracy and the United States Congress harbor the brunt of accountability for the effective abandonment of public education in the District, since public education in the nation's capital has operationally been relegated as another unformidable human service (Toyer 2003).

Furthermore, with respect to substandard leadership and flagrant mismanagement, paltry funding is a key, albeit, not the principal, cause for poor academic achievement as some proclaim. While ample funding is central to student academic performance, *Children in Crisis* revealed that appropriate budget planning was not adequately considered in preparing the annual DCPS budget (Children in Crisis 1996). Essentially, the DCPS has consistently submitted impracticable and inadequate budget requests to the United States Congress. Consequently, the DCPS has forcibly diverted millions of dollars from line-items to compensate for personnel and administrative costs. Subsequently, given that the District's public school system does not receive the total funding for operation, the DCPS cannot provide requisite funding for teacher retention and recruitment, infrastructure improvement, or delivery of critical programs (Sarnoff 2004). Hence, limited caches of funding strain established and innovative vehicles that rouse student academic progress, thereby alleviating *some* accountability on behalf of the DCBE and Superintendents. However, in the face of funding controls, DC's educational leaders are solely responsible for unmonitored spending and the lack of administrative oversight that negatively affect academic performance.

Despite the shortcomings of school officials and bureaucrats, and inadequate funding, controversy regarding the DCOSP is a litigious quarrel over funding, home rule, public demand and politics. From a funding standpoint, it has been argued that the least efficient way to use federal dollars is to hand to a few individuals when the same amount could help many more children (Norton 2003). Specifically, given that school choice promotes competition, it is categorically dishonest not to provide DCPS the tools and funding necessary to compete (Cafritz 2003). Likewise, albeit done historically disgraceful, many have contended that the federal government's violation of "home rule" regarding the management of the District's public education system is decisively unjust. Furthermore, since most District voters are opposed to federally-funded school vouchers for low-income residents implies that District constituents covet educational reform through other means.

Although bureaucrats and elected officials continuously deny that the DCOSP is politically motivated, qualitative analysis informs otherwise. Additionally, "it is not even remotely conceivable that Congress would impose a voucher program in Houston or Miami if the Texas or Florida congressional delegates opposed the program" (Toyer 2003). Thus, based on the fact that the District does not have an active congressional vote leaves the District vulnerable to a five-year federally funded experiment rather than converging on inherent accountability standards and performance measures outlined in NCLB.

Granted, the implementation of NCLB without anticipated funding has applied extreme pressure on DC's bureaucracy and public school officials. However, since its enactment, DCPS has effectively restructured itself in order to meet stringent accountability standards and performance measures as outlined in NCLB. In an effort to meet academic benchmarks, the new Superintendent of DCPS, Clifford Janey, has appointed 414 principals. Likewise, 800 teachers without required credentials now exist, a dramatic decrease from 1,400 teachers (Haynes 2005). Given the aggressive approach to educational reform in the District, many have reservations about the necessity and legitimacy of federally-funded vouchers. Furthermore, NCLB data indicate that implemented accountability measures and performance standards are positively affecting academic performance. In essence, preliminary evidence suggests that the DCOSP was employed impulsively based on political agendas and religious beliefs without forethought of the potential outcomes of NCLB. But is this true? Were political strategies and dogma the buttress for the DC Opportunity Scholarship Program as described in the Consolidated Appropriations Act of 2004 without regard to the affect of NCLB in DCPS?

Data Analysis

The data collected for this study relate to the issues and questions presented in the introduction section of this chapter. Although the preceding perspectives contained in this investigation was largely based on congressional testimony and scrutiny by education policy analysts, the crux of these data demonstrated in this analysis derives from the 2004 Report on *Restoring Excellence to the District of Columbia Public Schools* and the *DCPS 2004–2005 No Child Left Behind Results: Annual Yearly Progress and Schools in Need of Improvement,* the Supreme Court decision in *Zellman v. Simmons-Harris,* and Congressional Roll Call votes of the District of Columbia Student Opportunity Scholarship Act of 1997, and the Consolidated Appropriations Act of 2004.

Restoring Excellence, in comparison to *Children in Crisis* as previously discussed in this chapter, analyzed the bureaucratic and internal factors that contributed to low academic performance. Likewise, the assessment and accountability results of the *DCPS 2004–2005 No Child Left Behind Results* report primarily focused on measuring achievement gaps between race and ethnicity: e.g., achievement gaps between White and Black students. However, this report, using the exact data contained in *DCPS 2004–2005 No Child Left Behind Results,* assesses reading and mathematical proficiency of students in the same race and ethnic subgroup from SY2003-04 to SY2004-05. This approach was chosen to determine if results would yield the same as those found in *DCPS 2004–2005 No Child Left Behind Results.*

In addition, *Zelman v. Simmons-Harris* as well as Congressional Roll Call votes were examined to determine if political ideology and religiosity were causal variables for the implementation of the first federally-funded school voucher program, notwithstanding the potential impressions NCLB have imposed on DCPS to improve student academic achievement. The District of Columbia Student Opportunity Scholarship Act of 1997 and the Consolidated Appropriations Act of 2004 are legislation that contained federal voucher programs for eligible District children. Thus, the objective here is to ascertain if certain causal relationships confirm the working hypothesis.

2004 Report, Restoring Excellence to the District of Columbia Public Schools

The findings of this report revealed that the DCBE had no formal mechanism for holding the Superintendent, principals, or senior instructional staff accountable for student performance (Restoring Excellence 2004). This investigation also found that the lack of accountability throughout the entire school system perpetuated an acceptable standard of contemptible student performance. Furthermore, this study verified that DCPS had no uniform plan for educators to guide instruction in reading and mathematics programs (Restoring Excellence 2004). Consequently, incoherent and compounded curricula augmented by disparate teaching strategies contributed to low reading and mathematical proficiency. In addition, the systemic problems with procurement, facilities, information technology, code words for dysfunction and mismanagement as Superintendent Clifford Janey declared in the 2005 DCPS Strategic Plan, *Declaration of Education*, the District's school system has been wrought with poor standardized test scores, high drop-out rates, criminal behavior, and a decrepit infrastructure that were consistently accentuated by local media outlets. Hence, although the Control Board's report, *Children in Crisis* and the Council of the Great City School's *Restoring Excellence* differ in their own respect, collectively analyzed they exposed numerous internal controls that affected student academic achievement.

DCPS 2004–2005 No Child Left Behind Results: Annual Yearly Progress and Schools in Need of Improvement

Given that race and ethnicity are critical in measuring academic achievement as described in NCLB, it is imperative that the demographics of the student population enrolled in DCPS was foremost. Second, although poverty rates were not cumulatively described in the *DCPS 2004–2005 No Child Left Behind Results*, this report mentions the percentage of students receiving free or reduced price meals as a subtle notification that the DCPS student body, consisting of a large proportion of Black children, is very poor or living in families in poverty. Third, in contrast to the *DCPS*

2004–2005 No Child Left Behind Results that measured achievement proficiency gaps between race and ethnic subgroup, this analysis measures reading and mathematical proficiency within the same race and ethnic subgroup. Subsequently, the results will ultimately reveal if NCLB has proven effective in repairing academic achievement in the District's youth, as well as determining the necessity of DCOSP. The racial and ethnic identity of DCPS student population is contained in Table 1, in which minorities consist of an estimated 95% of the student body.

According to U.S. Census Bureau data, almost one-third of DCPS children in families lived in poverty from 1998 to 2002. The historical time-series analysis shown in Table 2 demonstrates decreases of DCPS children in families living in poverty from 1998 to 2000. However, this analysis reveals that DCPS children living in poverty dramatically increased in 2001. This dramatic increase can logically be explained as a change or interruption in the presidential administration and subsequent economic policies.

Using student eligibility for free or reduced meals as another means to measure poverty in DCPS, Chart 1 demonstrates a range from 52% to 78% of DCPS children, pre-kindergarten through grade 12, that received free or reduced price meals in School Year 2004–2005. Thus, according to this measure, an average of 63% of DCPS children resides in low income households or families in poverty. Although the impact of poverty on student academic achievement is miniscule as concluded in a recent Minnesota study (Myers 2004), and this report, the high concentration of DCPS children living in destitution is relevant to this analysis given that the long-term impact of NCLB obviously affects minorities because they make-up 95% of the student body. In essence, those same minority children, particularly Blacks, based on free or reduced price meal measure, are likely to be living in low income households or families in poverty.

Table 1: Race/Ethnicity of DCPS Student Population

Race/Ethnicity	Student Population	Percentage
Black	52,094	83.61
White	3,028	4.86
Hispanic	6,075	9.75
Asian/Pac Islander	1,077	1.73
Native American	32	0.05
Total	62,306	100.00

Source: *DCPS 2004–2005 No Child Left Behind Results* found on http://www.k12.dc.us/dcps/home.html

Table 2: DCPS Children in Families Living in Poverty

Year	Age 5–17 in Families Living in Poverty	Percent of Age 5–17 Living In Poverty	Percent Change
2002	21,767	29.8	—
2001	20,583	27.1	9.96
2000	21,067	27.5	-1.45
1999	22,906	28.1	-2.14
1998	21,266	30.2	-6.95

Source: http://www.census.gov/cgi-bin/saipe/saipe.cgi

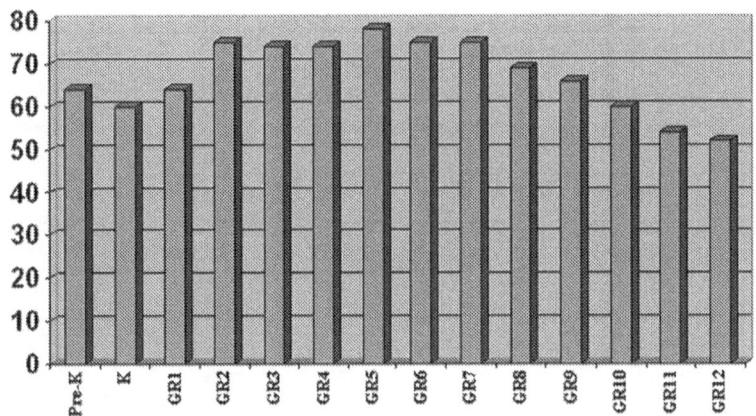

Figure 1: 2004–2005 Eligibility Data For Free and Reduced Price Meals
(Percentage)
Source: *DCPS 2004–2005 No Child Left Behind Results* found on
http://www.k12.dc.us/dcps/home.html

With the impact of NCLB criterion as a means to improve student academic achievement, student performance in this report measures proficiency gains in the same race and ethnic subgroup from the elementary to secondary school level between SY2003-04 to SY2004-05. Disaggregate results by each ethnic subgroup at the elementary school level reflect improvements in reading, especially among Black and Hispanic students (Table 3). In mathematics, proficiency gains were achieved by all ethnic subgroups as well (Table 4).

Table 3: DCPS Elementary School Proficiency Gains in Reading

Ethnic Subgroup	Percentage Proficiency		Percentage Proficiency Difference
	SY03-04	SY04-05	
White	89.2	90.0	0.90
Black	43.8	47.4	8.22
Hispanic	44.3	51.2	15.56
Asian	72.8	72.9	0.14

Source: *DCPS 2004–2005 No Child Left Behind Results* found on http://www.k12.dc.us/dcps/home.html

Table 4: DCPS Elementary School Proficiency Gains in Mathematics

Ethnic Subgroup	Percentage Proficiency		Percentage Proficiency Difference
	SY03-04	SY04-05	
White	90.3	90.9	0.66
Black	52.8	54.5	3.22
Hispanic	61.9	67.2	8.56
Asian	87.2	89.0	2.06

Source: *DCPS 2004–2005 No Child Left Behind Results* found on http://www.k12.dc.us/dcps/home.html

Table 5: DCPS Secondary School Proficiency Gains in Reading

Ethnic Subgroup	Percentage Proficiency		Percentage Proficiency Difference
	SY03-04	SY04-05	
White	81.0	79.7	-1.60
Black	28.9	27.4	-5.19
Hispanic	27.5	28.9	5.09
Asian	44.6	46.0	3.14

Source: *DCPS 2004–2005 No Child Left Behind Results* found on http://www.k12.dc.us/dcps/home.html

Table 6: DCPS Secondary School Proficiency Gains in Mathematics

Ethnic Subgroup	Percentage Proficiency		Percentage Proficiency Difference
	SY03-04	SY04-05	
White	82.6	80.2	-2.91
Black	33.8	28.3	-16.27
Hispanic	42.4	42.5	0.24
Asian	79.5	77.4	-2.64

Source: *DCPS 2004–2005 No Child Left Behind Results* found on http://www.k12.dc.us/dcps/home.html

Student academic achievement at the secondary school level reveals decreases in reading proficiency among White and Black students, and improvements by Hispanic and Asian students. Disaggregate results by ethnic subgroups are shown in (Table 5). Similarly, mathematical proficiency declined among White, Black, and Asian students. The data indicate a minute increase among Hispanic students (Table 6).

In addition to gains or reductions by ethnic subgroups in reading and mathematics, this report discloses accountability results according to the new State Accountability Plan for DCPS. This accountability plan indicates the number of years and the number of schools failing to achieve

Adequate Yearly Progress (AYP). According to the 2005 DCPS Strategic Plan, *Declaration of Education,* schools identified as Targeted Assistance receive additional assistance and intervention to prevent them from being classified as Schools In Need of Improvement. Schools identified as In Need of Improvement receive substantial, effective, school-based intervention strategies from the DCPS (Declaration of Education 2005). According to the Strategic Plan, this entails additional training for teachers and curriculum-based strategies for each child (Declaration of Education 2005). Schools that failed to meet AYP for three consecutive years are categorized as Schools In need of Corrective Action. Schools in this classification are subject to decrease management authority, an outside advisor, extended school days or school year, and staff reformation (Declaration of Education 2005). Finally, schools that do not meet AYP for four repeated years or more are categorized as Schools In Need of Restructuring. Those with this label are prone to have their operations outsourced under state management. Schools identified in their appropriate classifications in Table 7 demonstrate an increase in schools failing to meet NCLB required AYP benchmarks from SY2004-05 to SY2005-06, especially in Schools in Need of Corrective Action.

Table 7: DCPS Accountability Results of SY2004-05 and SY2005-06

DC Accountability Plan Categories	Years Failing To Make AYP	Number of Schools Identified Under New DC Accountability Plan	
		SY2004-05	SY2005-06
Incentive Schools	NA	61	59
Targeted Assistance	1	21	12
Schools In Need of Improvement	2	51	37*
Schools In Need of Corrective Action	3	8	31
Schools In Need of Restructuring—Year 1	4	8	6

Schools In Need of Restructuring—Year 2	5	0	6
Total Schools	-----	149	151**

Source: *DCPS 2004–2005 No Child Left Behind Results* found on http://www.k12.dc.us/dcps/home.html

* Two schools are classified as In Need of Improvement due to attendance
** In cases where sufficient data were not available (less than 40 students), the accountability status remained the same as SY2004-05.

Zelman v. Simmons-Harris, 436 U.S. (2002)

In *Zelman v. Simmons-Harris*, the United States Supreme Court held in a 5-4 vote that the City of Cleveland was not in violation of the Establishment Clause that effectively affirms the separation between church and state. The issue in this legal action rests on whether Cleveland's voucher program systematically advanced religion with government funding. The majority opinion written by Chief Justice William Rehnquist, held that Cleveland's voucher program passed constitutional muster because it is "neutral" and public funds flow religious schools only as the result of "private choice" of parents (People for the American Way 2004). Hence, parents that received school vouchers for their children to advance their children academically were essentially given a choice between secular and religious schools. In contrast, the dissenting opinion objected to *any* public funds to support parochial educational programs by religious institutions (Destro 2002).

Although the dissenters and the majority in *Zelman* reached different conclusions based on their perceptions (Hamilton 2002), the most conspicuous regarding this decision is that it was made along party lines, with Justice Sandra Day O'Connor casting the swing vote. However, despite the justification that the United States Supreme Court held in *Zelman*, it is plausible to conclude that the majority reached its decision based on religion and political ideology. Consequently, the decision held in *Zelman* arguably set legal precedent for the first enacted federally-funded school voucher program, the DC Opportunity Scholarship Program contained in the Consolidated Appropriations Act of 2004.

Congressional Roll Call Votes

Using data from Congressional Roll Call Votes in two key legislative acts that included federally funded voucher programs, the chronological time-series data measured by roll call votes in S. 1502, the District of Columbia Student Opportunity Scholarship Act of 1997, and H.R. 2673, the Consolidated Appropriations Act of 2004 indicates that they were effectively decided based on political ideology. With the United States Senate consisting of 55 Republicans and 45 Democrats in the 105th Congress, bill S. 1502 passed due to a Unanimous Consent Agreement. Under the same bill, the House of Representatives adopted S. 1502 as House Resolution 413 (Table 8), and it passed along party lines in favor of the Republican Party. Specifically, 94% of participating Republicans in the House voted for this measure. However, when this legislation reached the Oval Office, President Bill Clinton vetoed The District of Columbia Student Opportunity Scholarship Act.

Similarly, the Congressional Roll Call votes for the Consolidated Appropriations Act, H.R. 2763, yielded a partisan return in the House of Representatives as shown in Table 9. Specifically, 83% of participating Republicans in the House voted for this legislation. In contrast, 70% of able Democrats in the House voted against the Consolidated Appropriations Act of 2004.

In the Senate, Republican roll call votes were decisive as shown in Table 10. Specifically, 92% Republicans voted for this act. However, the Senate vote for this measure was equally divided among Democrats with 45% voting in favor of this legislation. Hence, political party identification can logically be perceived as the determinant factor for the first enacted federally-funded voucher program.

Table 8: House of Representative Roll Call Votes for the District of Columbia Student Opportunity Scholarship Act of 1997

	YES	NO	PRES	NOT VOTING
REPUBLICAN	208	13	1	5
DEMOCRAT	6	192	—	7
INDEPENDENT	—	1	—	—
TOTAL	214	206	1	12

Source: http://thomas.loc.gov/home/rollcallvotes.html

Table 9: House of Representative Roll Call Votes for the Consolidated Appropriations Act of 2004

	YES	NO	PRES	NOT VOTING
REPUBLICAN	184	38	. —	7
DEMOCRAT	58	137	—	10
INDEPENDENT	—	1	—	—
TOTAL	242	176	—	17

Source: http://thomas.loc.gov/home/rollcallvotes.html

Table 10: Senate Roll Call Votes for the Consolidated Appropriations Act of 2004

	YES	NO	PRES	NOT VOTING
REPUBLICAN	44	4	—	3
DEMOCRAT	21	23	—	4
INDEPENDENT	—	1	—	—
TOTAL	65	28	—	7

Source: http://thomas.loc.gov/home/rollcallvotes.html

To demonstrate a causal model of the variables contained in this analysis, a path diagram shown in Figure 1 illustrates logical sequences to confirm the hypothesis. Given the precedent-setting *Zelman* decision, Z1 to Z3 to Z4 to Z5 is the logical path for the enactment of DCOSP.

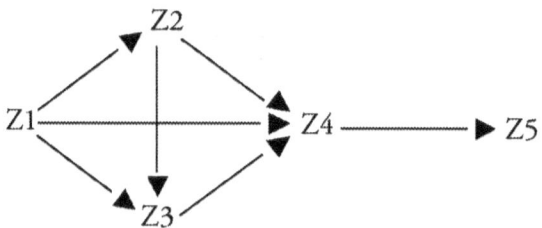

Z5 = President Bush's Approval
Z4 = Congressional Roll Call Votes of Consolidated Appropriates Act 0f 2004 (that includes the DCOSP)
Z3 = *Zelman v. Simmons-Harris* (2002)
Z2 = Congressional Roll Call Votes of DC Student Opportunity Scholarship Act (vetoed by President Clinton in 1998)
Z1 = Political Ideology/Party Identification

Figure 1: Path Diagram for the Enactment of DCOSP

Discussion of Results

In comparison to the Control Board's 1996 report *Children in Crisis,* as discussed previously in this chapter, *Restoring Excellence* confirmed that deficient academic performance of the District's children was predominantly based on an absent coherent, comprehensive strategic plan inherent with objectives and methodologies to enhance student academic achievement. Likewise, this report concluded that absent leadership and mismanagement were cardinal factors that crippled the District's public education system. Granted, arguments insist that behavior from DCPS children in families living in poverty extract from effective teaching to maintain discipline, order, and attend to children expressing home and familial problems (Myers 2004). However, the lack of focus and low expectations from teachers, principals, and superintendents' alike, perpetuated acceptable benchmarks of poor performance despite the astounding levels of DCPS children deemed to be living in low-income households or families in poverty described earlier. As a result, most DCPS students, in particular Blacks were not induced or compelled to achieve proficiency levels of performance comparable to their White counterparts. Hence, the *Children in Crisis* assessment that each additional year that students stay in DCPS, the less likely they are to succeed, not because they are unable to succeed, but because the system does not prepare them to succeed is precise, especially pertaining to the majority Black student population in DCPS (Children in Crisis 1996). Further, considering the gross number of Black students enrolled in DCPS, the same result can be derived from *Restoring Excellence*. Moreover, the sharp decrease in reading and mathematic proficiency among Black students from the elementary to secondary school level found in the *DCPS 2004–2005 No Child Left Behind Results* indicate that Black students remain deficient despite NCLB's progressive subject matter benchmarks.

Given that the NCLB is flawed in many respects, the achievement and accountability standards imposed on District school officials and educators revealed the inefficiency and ineffectiveness of the District's governance in public education. More importantly, the NCLB systematically holds the District's educational leadership and teachers directly accountable for incremental standards to advance student academic achievement. However, NCLB measures have yet to prove that they are effective remedies in repairing student performance, necessary or even beneficial due to the inadequate funding and unattainable benchmarks imposed on officials and educators. Although the NCLB helped expose the ineptitude and negligence of the District's educational leadership, teachers, and support service staff alike in the short-term, this mandate is still in the early stages. Thus, the findings in NCLB required Adequate Yearly Progress reports to date cannot demonstrate a sustainable impact on student performance in District schools. In addition, current Superintendent Clifford B. Janey's salient changes are in its infancy, therefore, an effective evaluation of his revisions cannot be performed as well.

Despite the potential outcomes of NCLB, congressional records and roll call votes demonstrate that the initial federally funded voucher bill passed in both chambers of Congress prior to the enactment of NCLB. Hence, the DCOSP was not launched impulsively as suggested earlier in this chapter. However, political ideology and agenda have been the underlying factor for partisan support for the DCOSP. Thus, the hypothesis is true, in which the support for the DCOSP that was effectively decided along party lines without regard to the impact of NCLB in DCPS.

Given that Republicans in both chambers of Congress endorsed the D.C. Student Opportunity Scholarship Act ahead of President Clinton's veto, and against the intense opposition by Democratic representatives, it is logical to presume that the Consolidated Appropriation Act of 2004, and the *Zelman* decision were all decided based on political ideology and religiosity. Since the Republican Party sanctioned the use of federal funds for school vouchers for top performing schools, namely parochial institutions. First year results of the DCOSP conclude that 51 percent of private schools participating in the program are affiliated with the Roman Catholic Church, and 21 percent are affiliated with non-Catholic religions (Evaluation of the DC 2005). Thus far, the Catholic Church undoubtedly has been the largest beneficiary of DCOSP (Kennedy 2001).

Conclusion

Presently, the primary avenue to countering the expansion of federally-funded voucher programs, such as the DCOSP, is advance student academic achievement in accordance with NCLB assessment and accountability benchmarks in the District's public schools despite the enormous challenge of reduced funding. Given that the DCOSP serves as the foundation for other potential federally funded voucher programs, the long-term results at the end of this experiment will effectively compare to NCLB AYP reports to determine future viability. Thus, it is imperative that the District's educational leadership emphasize and improve student performance to detract the appeal to privatize public education, and expanding achievement gaps between District White children and handful of Blacks, and minority youth that overwhelmingly live in poverty. Granted, the NCLB is imperfect with unreasonable expectations. However, it is critical that Superintendent Janey's reform measures linked to NCLB expectations prove to be effective. Otherwise, a *legal* disparity between public and private institutions will be created, gradually reverting to a separate and unequal education in District that served as the premise for *Brown v. Board of Education.*

10

The No Child Left Behind Act

✦

Autumn Saxton-Ross

Introduction

Early models of communication and evaluation networks for education came out of the common schools of New England, specifically Massachusetts, Ohio and Connecticut (Warren 1974). By the late 1830s, proposals delineating a central education agency began appearing, with the main objectives of collecting and disseminating educational statistics, to publicize individual and social improvement from increased educational opportunity. Established in 1867, amidst much opposition and controversy, the Department of Education came into existence to standardize American education and to increase the educational opportunities for the freedmen of the South. Not much unlike the implementation of the Freedman's Bureau, good intentions did not transfer into practical application and equal opportunity.

On January 23, 2001, President George W. Bush announced his number one domestic priority as education, which was manifested in the No Child Left Behind (NCLB) plan for comprehensive education reform (US Department of Education 2005). Nothing innovative, the NCLB was a 'revitalization' of the Elementary and Secondary Education Act of 1965 (ESEA), which provided local school districts with additional funds to meet the needs of "special populations" and "educationally deprived children." Passed during the Johnson Administration, the ESEA was a successor to Roosevelt's' Great Society programs, attempting to lessen the adversities of poverty. The ESEA acknowledged the disparities in educational achievement observed between Blacks and Whites, and those of high and low-income, through the use of the National Assessment of Educational Progress (NAEP) (Kafer 2004).

Using three decades of data, the NAEP has tracked the trends of achievement gaps; and in 2003, it found that by income levels, 16 percent of low-income eight graders were proficient in reading and 12 percent in math, while about three times as many higher-income students were proficient at grade level (Kafer 2004). During the 1990s and early 21st Century, the ESEA and its additional programs had evolved, including the new educational discourse of accountability through standardized testing. With the re-enactment in 1994 to receive Title I funding, states would have to establish academic standards, centered on reading and math proficiency, and publish disaggregated analyses, reporting the progress of disadvantaged students. Those states with high accountability standards, sanctions and rewards that improved achievement, with the help of research, reinforced the notion of achievement and accountability through increased testing. Even with accountability trends, by the end of the Clinton Administration, barley 20 percent of the states were in compliance, although all received funding (Kafer 2004).

The No Child Left Behind Act, 2001

Using the NCLB, the Bush Administration sought to tighten restrictions and regulations through state and local accountability, requiring states to test all students annually in grades 3–8 in reading and mathematics, and report scores in disaggregated data by race, gender, socioeconomic status, disability, and English proficiency. This plan, based on four principles—(1) stronger accountability for results, (2) expanded flexibility for local control, (3) increased options for parents and children, and (4) emphasizing proven teaching methods—is the largest education reform plan since the Civil Rights Act of 1964 (which provided the federal support and implementation of Brown 1954) and the Elementary and Secondary Education Act of 1965. Once passed, the bill was not much dissimilar to prior reenactments; it just entailed additional accountability measures. The four major objectives of the NCLB are as follows:

1. *Increased Accountability for Results:* According to President Bush, the NCLB Act will strengthen Title I accountability by requiring states to implement accountability systems for public schools and students, based on standards for reading and mathematics, with annual state-wide progress reports. These data must be separated by poverty status, race, ethnicity, disability and English proficiency to ensure that 'no child is left behind.' Districts and schools that do not achieve adequate yearly progress (AYP) will receive corrective restructuring action aimed at assisting them to meet the statewide goals. Those that meet AYP objectives are eligible for awards in the form of increased flexibility in the spending and transfer of federal funds.

2. *Increased Options for Parents and Students:* Students attending Title 1 schools that fail to meet these state standards and AYP goals have the opportunity to attend better public schools, where transportation is provided by the district, or the use of federal funds to obtain supplementary educational services from public or private sector providers (only if the school has consistently failed for 3–4 years, and the child is from a low-income family).

3. *Greater Flexibility for Local Control:* The flexibility provisions in the NCLB Act give state and local districts the authority to transfer up to 50% of funding received under four major state grant programs to any one of the programs or to Title 1.

4. *Emphasizing Proven Educational Methods:* Through the President's Reading First Initiative, the NCLB Act attempts to ensure that every child can read by the end of the third grade by increasing the federal investment in scientifically based reading instruction programs in the primary grades. This legislation also attempts to make it easier for local schools to recruit qualified teachers.

From educators, parents to politicians, there are many conflicting views on the efficacy of such a large-scale reform. Many agree with the goals of the policy—to create higher national standards for all children, meet the needs of disadvantaged children, recruit well qualified teachers, and educational accountability measures for states and school systems. But, the disagreement on NCLB comes from the way that the policy is implemented (McElroy 2005). Aside from the lack of funding to support these lofty wishes, there are many underlying structural issues dealing with quality and equity within the education system (among others) as a whole that this policy seems not to address (Gray 2004).

Through an observation of gender, race, education budget (in weighted and deflated 2004 dollars) and Title I eligibility as they relate to DC test scores three years after the passing of NCLB through school year 2004–2005, this chapter examines the effects of this reform on minority children's test scores within a school district, The District of Columbia's Public School system (DCPS), with a population that is 95% "minority."

Review of Existing Perspectives

Since the passage of this law, there has been an ever growing debate about the validity, accountability and plausibility of the NCLB's most idealistic goal–to close the achievement gap between minority students and their white counterparts, which is a disparity that has existed since the creation of the Department of Education. Emerging from the literature, whether political, academic or popular, various perspectives have arisen. But even within these works, DCPS, a public school system comprised mostly of minority students, is rarely mentioned or discussed. This chapter reviews the existing works as they relate to the agreement or disagreement of the NCLB.

Educational Funding: Title I Eligibility and Implementation

Not soon after NCLB was passed, the media flooded public opinion inciting approval as a result of the bipartisan passage of this law. Due to the shear size of it, NCLB is one of the most complicated pieces of education legislation, quite often creating confusion in its interpretation.

Jay Mathews, a *Washington Post* Staff writer, attempted to dismiss many myths that were circulated throughout mass media. One of the most common myths was that with this law, the federal government was spending more than ever on education. In 2003, government spending on education was at about 7% of the total budget, where the majority comes from state and local administrations. With this, local administrations are forced to spend that money for transportation and additional administrative staffing, not the essential resources needed to implement the new NCLB regulations. Hackney Gray (2004) noted that in Bush's 2004 presidential debate, he stated that federal funding for education had been increased by 40%. The question to the validity of this statement is whether inflation, and the value of the dollar as if fluctuates over the year, is taken into account.

Title I Eligibility

The Title I program provides federal funds to states and school districts for the education of disadvantaged children (Fagan 2005). Under NCLB, states are required to test and report disaggregated student progress and submit plans that show how students' performances will improve each year, with the objective of accomplishing 100 percent proficiency in math and reading in 12 years. Districts must allow students attending Title I schools that have not met AYP standards for two years the opportunity to register in better performing schools. According to the Children's Defense Fund (2004), the current administration's funding for Title I is $7.1 billion below what was promised in the President's education bill. One of the major concerns with the NCLB and Title I funding is if districts with higher percentages of minority students will receive the monetary support necessary to decrease the disparities observed between other ethnic groups and White achievement.

When speaking of Title I eligibility, the fundamental issue that determines eligibility is the percentage of the student population that is at a social and economic disadvantage. According to Hackney Gray (2004), the mean reading score of a student can be predicted by the aggregate rates of childhood poverty and other social ills or, in other words, the more a school's students are from poor, urban neighborhoods, the worse (on average) the students perform. Within the District of Columbia system, over 80% of the schools, roughly 160 schools, receive Title I funding. The notion of Title I eligibility not only speaks to the issue of adequate funding, but also to equitable resources and education, and the need to focus on early education instead of early testing.

NCLB Implementation

With the nonpartisan passage of NCLB, most officials, administrators, teachers and parents were supportive of the intent to raise standards and improve teacher qualifications, but some feel that the goal of total proficiency by 2014 is too lofty (Pinkerton, Kober, Scott & Buell 2003). Pinkerton, Kober, Scott and Buell (2003), with assistance from the Center on Education Policy, commissioned a case study of 15 districts' implementation of NCLB and found that in most states experiencing budget restraints, there are questions as to whether there will be adequate financial support to carry NCLB's complex implementation. The Children's Defense Fund (2004) noted that over a year, the increase within the education budget was at about 1.8 percent, while mandates, standards and tough accountability become increasingly complex. With the implementation of this law, states are required to do more testing, data collection, administration, and reporting. While the government is demanding 100% accountability, it is providing only 10% of the funds (Committee for Education Funding, 2004). Even with the consensus that nationwide school accountability can be a good thing, the question of if there has (and will be) adequate and appropriate funding to improve test scores has not.

Nationwide "Standards" for Adequate Yearly Progress

Federal law gives each state the freedom to set standards and to choose and create tests. This creates differing measures, state to state, as to what is "adequate" progress and what is not. So, a fifth grader within a Midwest district school that has tested as proficient may not be considered the same in a Southern school district. These unstandardized regulations allow for discrepancies in ratings, and these inconsistencies have the possibility of undermining the accountability objective of the law (Kafer 2004, Matthews 2003).

Prior to the NCLB, many states were not required to disaggregate data by race, ethnicity, income, English language learners, and students with disabilities. This requirement has the potential to benefit many districts, allowing them a true representation of the learning curves within their student populations (Pinkerton, Kober, Scott & Buell 2003). But, through the NCLB's focus on reading and math, many educators believe that today's students are at an educational disadvantage. To achieve statewide AYP goals, many districts must cut theatre, art, music and physical education programs to manage the fiscal and personnel demands now required by NCLB. In a nationally representative survey administered by the Center on Educational Policy (2005), one quarter of all districts have reduced somewhat or to a great extent their instructional time in other traditional subjects. To many, this all too common practice ultimately affects the students, stifling creativity and exposure, and preventing success in subjects other reading and math.

Within the past three decades, there has been increasingly more attention given to the assertion that the majority of standardized tests are culturally biased in content and they way that the results are used (Green & Griffore 1980). According to Green and Griffore, test bias is present when a test does not measure the same dimension(s) of achievement across different groups and is commonly referred to when plausible explanations in achievement gaps across differing groups are proposed. The central argument is that the content (linguistics, semantics and vocabulary) of standardized tests are associated more with individuals of higher socioeconomic status; therefore, those children of lower-income parents and neighborhoods are predisposed to lower scores. Considering that 20% of Washington, DC's student population is below the poverty level, not including those at or just above the poverty level, how does increased standardized testing account for the possibility of cultural and economic bias in testing? Or, even more importantly, does high standardized test scores really show achievement and predict success?

Data Collection

When budgets are compared, quite often there is an assumption that the value of the US dollar remains constant over the years. One way to take into account the fluctuation in the value of currencies and the effect of inflation on those values is through the use of the Consumer Price Index (CPI) (Fixler 1993). The CPI is produced by the Bureau of Labor Statistics and serves as an approximation of the ideal cost of living index, and it is a measure of the average change in prices paid by urban consumers for a fixed market basket of goods and services (Fixler 1993). The CPI is used when calculating many economic indicators that require constant dollar measures like estimates of income, earnings and poverty (Stewart & Reed 1999). Constant dollar figures are estimates representing an effort to remove the effects of price changes, resulting in figures that would presumably exist if prices were the same according to the base year (2004), as if the dollar had constant purchasing power (US Census Bureau 2004).

Table 1: Elementary and Secondary Education Budget

Total Elementary and Secondary Education Budget: President's Budget*		
School Year	Budget	Budget in Constant 2004 Dollars**
2001–2002	$ 28,681,510	$ 30,127, 058
2002–2003	$ 33,006,176	$ 33,890,741
2003–2004	$ 34,204,076	$ 34,204,076

*from the US Education Department's Budget by Major Program
**constant 2004 dollar amounts were estimated by multiplying the budget amount for each respective year by the product of the CPI-2004 divided by the CPI for that year, made available from http://www.census.gov/hhes/www/income/income04/cpiurs.html

When speaking of the education budget, which includes teachers salaries, building maintenance, transportation costs, and supplies (which are prices governed by the market), it is important to take into account these changes, comparing increases in constant dollars, as they affect the actual amount spent within a given school's walls for implementation of NCLB objectives and per pupil spending. The assumption made is that increases in the US Department of Education's budget includes the above estimates and, if so, that an appropriate amount is appropriated to account for the added expense of adhering to the NCLB's objectives of increased accountability and increased options for parents and students. According to the Center on Educational Policy (CEP), for the fiscal year of 2005, the 3% increase in Title I funding will not keep pace with the 6% rise in the number of children in poverty, making less money available to those in need the most. In 1999, 20% of the District's families were below the poverty level. Within the DCPS education budget, 23% of the yearly allotment is for state functions (money that the District directly controls); and of that, over 95% is spent on Special Education programs, tuition, and transportation (Franzese & Osueke 2004).

Table 2: The District of Columbia's Average Math and Reading Scores: SY 2002

School Year 2002*		Average Math Scores		Average Reading Scores	
Race	Gender	Title I	No Title I	Title I	No Title I
Black	Female	626.35	673.50	630.83	676.59
	Male	620.78	659.43	622.09	658.31
Hispanic	Female	624.75	673.18	623.67	670.94
	Male	627.74	661.49	621.98	657.23
White	Female	705.84	685.46	706.38	692.20
	Male	688.72	695.46	704.05	684.40

*information from http://nces.ed.gov/nationsreportcard/states/profile.asp

Table 3: The District of Columbia's Average Math and Reading Scores: SY 2003

School Year 2003*		Average Math Scores		Average Reading Scores	
Race	**Gender**	**Title I**	**No Title I**	**Title I**	**No Title I**
Black	Female	637.2	677.66	639.43	680.06
	Male	631.09	663.99	630.01	662.47
Hispanic	Female	631.07	677.75	627.98	676.78
	Male	631.17	670.22	624.29	659.56
White	Female	708.35	708.59	711.02	711.53
	Male	718.59	712.28	707.98	705.27

*information from http://nces.ed.gov/nationsreportcard/states/profile.asp

Table 4: The District of Columbia's Average Math and Reading Scores: SY 2004

School Year 2004*		Average Math Scores		Average Reading Scores	
Race	**Gender**	**Title I**	**No Title I**	**Title I**	**No Title I**
Black	Female	638.75	673.01	641.85	674.28
	Male	632.57	655.11	632.65	655.67
Hispanic	Female	635.07	676.96	632.36	677.92
	Male	636.04	674.22	629.07	668.35
White	Female	709.36	709.82	711.28	714.45
	Male	721.38	711.65	713.14	708.57

* Information from http://nces.ed.gov/nationsreportcard/states/profile.asp

As of 2004, the No Child Left Behind AYP data rank DCPS schools as low performing and ranked last out the 50 school districts according to the National Assessment for Educational Progress (NAEP).

Data Analysis

According to the US Census Bureau, The District of Columbia's 2004 population estimate is 553,523, of whom 20.1% are under the age of 18. Sixty percent of the District's total population is Black or African American; and of the total population, as of 1999 data, 20.2 % of District residents were at or below the poverty level.

In 2004, the District of Columbia Public School system had approximately 78,057 students enrolled, 84% of whom are Black or African American, 9% Hispanic/Latino, 4.6% Caucasian/White, and 1.6% Asian (Figure 1). Within the school district, there are a total of 207 schools, with an average per-pupil expenditure of $11,968 and a 13.8 pupil-to-teacher ratio. Over 80% of the District's schools receive Title I funding.

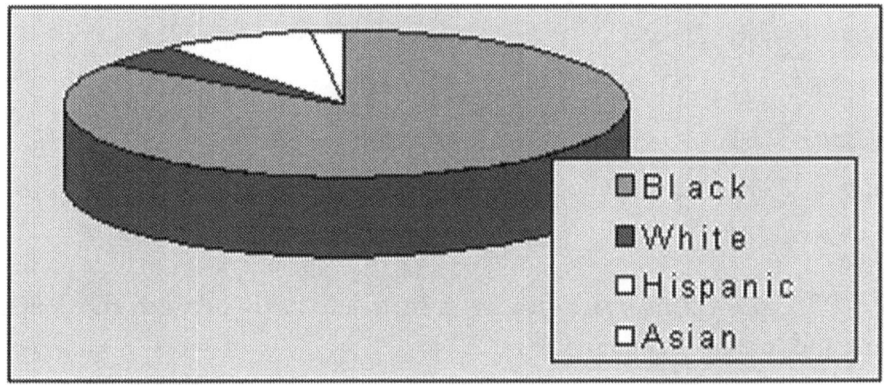

Figure 1: DCPS Students by Race (in Percentages)

Multiple regression analysis is a set of statistical techniques that allows one to assess the relationship between one dependent variable and several independent variables. For the purposes of the study, the dependent variable examined comprises students' test scores in math and reading; and the independent variables are gender, race, Title I eligibility, and education budget. The result of this type of analysis is a regression equation that represents the best prediction of student test scores (Y), taking into account Title I eligibility (χ_1), gender (χ_2), race (χ_3), and education budget (χ_4).

$$Y= \alpha +\beta\chi_1+\beta\chi_2+\beta\chi_3+\beta\chi_4+ \varepsilon$$

Table 5: Multiple Regression Results of Reading and Math Scores

Multiple Regression: Average DC Reading and Math Scores

Reading Scores			Math Scores		
Independent Variable(s)	Beta	Significance	Independent Variable(s)	Beta	Significance
Title I	.389	.001*	Title I	.342	.002*
Gender	.124	.234	Gender	.036	.730
Race	.713	.000*	Race	.742	.000*
Education Budget	.067	.773	Education Budget	.131	.572
R^2 = .688			R^2 = .688		
Adjusted R^2 = .635			Adjusted R^2 = .636		
F score = 13.201			F score = 13.222		
Significance = .000*			Significance = .000*		

*P< .05, representing a significance in the relationship between the dependent and independent variables

Of the four factors examined in this study, looking to observe the relationship that Title I eligibility, gender, race and education budget have on reading and math test scores, only Title I eligibility and race have significant relationships with students' test scores. In other words, a student's test scores can be better predicted if Title I eligibility and the student's race is known.

The value of R^2 represents the amount of variance in the dependent variable that can be explained by the independent variable. In models that have only one independent variable, R^2 is used. In this research, the adjusted R^2 is used to explain the variability, because a relationship between multiple independent variables and one dependent variable was examined. When taking into account gender, race, Title I eligibility and education budget, 63.5% of the variance in reading scores and 63.6% of the variance in math scores is accounted for. Beta, or β, is a standardized constant representing the magnitude of the relationship between the respective independent and dependent variables. The standardized beta allows the results to be generalized to the population. According to the results, for reading scores, race (β= .713) and Title I eligibility (β=.389), and for math, race (β=.742) and Title I eligibility (β=.342) have the two greatest magnitudes.

Conclusion

When discussing the four major initiatives of NCLB, all sides agree on their importance within the education system. What the results of this research highlight is the need for adequate resources and analysis of what foundations actually support achievement.

Upon review of the initial data (Tables 2-4), an interesting trend with regards to Title I eligibility was highlighted. For students of minority status (Blacks and Hispanics), those that were tested in Title I schools consistently had lower averages in reading and math, for both male and female students (differences between 20 to 40 points), than those that were tested in schools that do not receive Title I funding. On average, the opposite was true of their White counterparts. In the year 2002 (Table 2), White females in Title I schools tested better than those in schools that did not receive Title I funding. For the years 2003 and 2004, White females in Title I schools, and those who were not had the same average reading (711.02 and 711.53 for 2003, 711.28 and 714.45 in 2004) and math scores (708.35 and 708.59 in 2003, 709.36 and 709.82 in 2004) regardless of Title I funding. For White males, on average, the same was true but not as obvious. This information suggests a more thorough analysis of what causes the learning differences in Title I and non-Title I schools as they relate to minority students education and learning. If the assumption is made that teachers are less competent in Title I schools, the fact that White students consistently excel in these schools shows that other influential variables within emphasizing proven teaching methods within NCLB deserve attention.

The DC Public School system, which over the past decade has been consistently ranked as one of the lowest performing systems, must begin to develop long-term plans to improve student achievement. The results of this research show that the allotted amount for education is not significant enough to initiate significant effects on reading and math test scores. For example, over half of the DCPS system's budget is spent on tuition and transportation for its special education population because the District does not have a working facility to educate some populations of children with special needs. If the city begins to refurbish one of the many vacant school buildings to service these children, how much money in the long run will be saved in tuition and transportation, and then re-filtered into educating the entire student population? A long-term plan such as this will create funds to increase the dollar amount that actually reaches the general student population.

According to the literature and mass media, political discourse has led most Americans to believe that the education budget has the most important effect on test scores; but within this model, race and Title I eligibility are of greater importance. One possible explanation as to why the education budget is not significant could be the amount allocated to the elementary and secondary schools' budget. The results suggest that the increases in the education budget have not been sufficient enough to improve reading and math scores. One of the added stresses to public education and the allotted budget is the increased administrative cost of NCLB, which takes an already over-extended budget and stretching it even thinner. When determining the education budget, administrators and politicians must first not only say that education is a number one priority in this country, but prove it, as action speaks louder than words. The education budget must be shaped around the changes in the purchasing power of the dollar, as to cover the services within educational systems, like salaries and basic materials to provide sufficient money, once those funds reach the class-room.

One important fact, which speaks to the core of NCLB, is that high standardized test scores do not equal improved learning or intelligence, represent achievement or predict success. When did accountability become synonymous with standardized test scores? Common knowledge (along with previous studies) have shown that many students with high SAT or ACT scores do not necessarily do better in college, and that higher standardized test scores are a more reliable measure of parental socioeco-nomic status. With this information, and the reality that these tests are culturally biased, how can increased testing in a system serving a 95% eth-nic minority population in which 20% are of lower SES expect signifi-cantly higher test scores? Educators, politicians and parents must use the increased flexibility for local control within NCLB to uncover diverse ways in which to measure achievement and learning, especially in those popula-tions that are now disaggregated under the law. Through the use of data that are reported according to race, disability, income, ethnicity and lan-guage, more varied and specific educational models can be employed and tested to find a better way to track achievement. Using one way to measure achievement does not account for different learning styles, promote active learning, or encourage higher order thinking. Accountability through stan-dardized reading and math test scores just continues the practice of rote learning–repetitiveness and memorization.

In a school system that serves a high population of ethnic minorities, specific strategies are necessary to elicit improved academic achievement. These approaches must address the issues of adequate support and resources, and find new ways of measuring achievement that translate across all groups.

Bibliography

Adam, R. 1982. "The Future of Teachers Union." *Comparative Education.* Vol. 12, No. 2; pp. 197-203.

Alt, Martha, N and Katharin Peter. 2002. *Private Schools: A Brief Report,* The Condition of Education American Federation of Teachers. 2006. "NCLB—Let's Get it Right." American Federation of Teachers; Washington, DC.

American University. 2006. "About the University." Washington DC: American University, Retrieved February 10, 2006 from www. american.edu

Archibald, George. January 29, 2004. "School Vouchers to Start by Fall." *The Washington Times.* Retrieved from http://www. washingtontimes.com

Archibald, George. March 5, 2004. "NEA Confirms Spending Audits." *The Washington Times.*

Arum, Richard. February 1996. "Do Private Schools Force Public Schools to Compete?" *American Sociological Review.* Vol. 61, No. 1; pp. 29-46

Author Unknown. 2006. *Schools in Need of Improvement for 2005-2006.* Retrieved March 14, 2006 from the World Wide Web: http://www.edreform.com

Balko, Radley. July 18, 2002. *Separate but Equal in Washington DC.* Retrieved from http://foxnews.com

Bass, Frank, Nicole Dizon and Ben Feller. May 2006. Schools Skirt, No Child Left Behind. *The Associated Press.*

Bangura, Abdul Karim, ed. 2005. *Washington, DC's Challenges.* Lincoln, NE: Writers Club Press.

Bangura, Abdul Karim, ed. 2003. *Washington, DC State of Affairs.* Lincoln, NE: Writers Club Press.

Bangura, Abdul Karim, ed. 2001. *DC Vote: Fighting Against Taxation Without Representation.* Lincoln, NE: Writers Club Press.

Bangura, Abdul Karim, ed. 2000. *Historical Political Economy of Washington, DC.* Lanham, MD: University Press of America.

Bangura, Abdul Karim and Mario D. Fenyo. 2003. *Law and Politics at the Grassroots: A Case Study of Prince George's County.* Lincoln, NE: iUniverse Press.

Basic Education Coalition. 1994. *Teach a Child: Transform a Nation.* Washington, DC: The Basic Education Coalition Publications.

Boehner, John. 2002. No Child Left Behind Transform Bilingual Education Program, Empowers Hispanic Parents to Ensure LEP Children Learn English. *Committee on Education and the Workforce.* Retrieved May 22, 2006.

Boehner, John. June 24, 2003. *School Choice in the District of Columbia: Opening Doors for Parents and Students.* Statement before the House of Representatives Committee on Government Reform. Retrieved from http://www.dcpswatch.com/vouchers/030624d.htm

Boren, Susan. August 28, 2003. "School Facilities Infrastructure: Background and Legislative roposals." *CRS Report for Congress.* The Library of Congress, Congressional Research Service: Washington, DC.

Brady, Thomas. February 8, 2006. "DC Public Schools: DC Council Approves One Billion C Schools." *The Washington Post.*

Bromley, Seth. March 23, 2006. Local School Officials Say No Child Left Behind Law is neffective, Unfair. *The Call.* Retrieved May 22, 2006.

Buckley, Jack, S. Kucsova and M. Schneider. 2003. "Building Social Capital in the Nation's apital: Can Charter Schools Build a Foundation for Cooperative Behavior?" *Washington DC Occasional Paper*, No. 82. National Center for the Study of Privatization in Education. Teachers College, Columbia University. Retrieved from www.ncspe. org

Buckley, Jack, M. Schneider and Y. Shang. 2004. "Are Charter School Students Harder to ducate?" *Washington DC Occasional Paper*, No. 69. National Center for the Study of Privatization in Education. Teachers College, Columbia University. Retrieved from www.ncspe. org

Butler, S.L.1987. "A Special Mission." *The National Education Association.* Washington DC: National Education Association

Cafritz, Peggy C. May 9, 2003. *In Search of Education Excellence in the Nation's Capital: A Review of Academic Options for Students and Parents in the District of Columbia.* Statement before the House of Representatives Committee on Government Reform.

Cane, Robert. December 17, 2001. *Misleading Statements on DC Education Funding.* Electronic communication sent to Peggy Cooper Cafritz, President of the DC Board of Education. Retrieved from http://www.focusdccharter.org/backgorund_issues/letters/121701cafritz.asp

Carnoy, Martin, R. Jacobsen, L. Mishel and R. Rothstein. March 2005. *The Charter School Dust-Up: Examining the Evidence on Enrollment and Achievement.* Economic Policy Institute Catholic University.

2006. "About Catholic University." Washington DC: Catholic University, Retrieved February 10, 2006 from www.cua.edu

Cavanagh, S. 2002. "Arizona Debates Moratorium on Vocational Districts." *Education Week*, Vol. 21, Issue 34; pp. 14-16

Center for Education Funding. 2004. "Education Budget Alert for Fiscal Year 2003." Washington, DC: Hackney Gray, R Center for Education Reform. "Washington DC Charter Law." Retrieved from http://www.edreform.com/index.cfm?fuseaction=claw&stateID=2

Center on Education Policy. July 2005. *NCLB: Narrowing the Curriculum?* NCLB Policy Brief Chavous, Kevin P. February 16, 2005. "Protecting Educational Opportunities for DC Kids." *The Center for Education Reform*: Washington DC.

Coleman, James, Thomas Hoffer and Sally Kilgore. April-July 1982. "Cognitive Outcomes in Public and Private Schools." *Sociology of Education*. Vol. 55, No. 2/3; pp. 65-76.

Clowes, George A. 1997. DC Voucher Still Alive in Congress. *School Reform News*. Chicago, IL: The Heartland Institute.

Congressional Record Service. 1998. Testimony to the House Committee on Appropriations Subcommittee in the District of Columbia. *Arlene Ackerman, Superintendent DC Public Schools*. June 24, 1998.

Congressional Record Service. 2003. Opening Statement of Chairman Tom Davis. Library of Congress: Speech on Government Reform, *Budget Autonomy for the District of Columbia: Restoring Trust in our Nation's Capital*. Rayburn House Office Building No. 2154, June 13, 2003.

Congressional Record Service. 2003. Introduction of DC Parental Choice Act of 2003. *Library of Congress: Speech of Honorable Tom Davis of Virginia, in the House of Representatives*. Article 3 of 4, June 23, 2003.

Congressional Record Service. 2004. Boehner Hails Senate Passage of Bipartisan DC School Choice Legislation. *Press Release, House Committee on Education and the Workforce.* Washington, DC. January 22, 2004.

Congressional Record Service. 2006. Federal Payment for School Improvement in theDistrict of Columbia. *Library of Congress: Senate Report 109-106—District of Columbia Appropriations Bill* Cooper, David E. April 25, 2002. "DC Public Schools Modernization Program Faces Major Challenges." Washington, DC: United States General Accounting Office.

Council of Great City Schools. January 2004. "Restoring Excellence to the District of Columbia Public Schools: Report of the Strategic Support Team of the Council of the Great City Schools. Retrieved from http://www.cgcs.org/taskforce/achievegap3/html

Davis, Tom. May 9, 2003. *In Search of Education Excellence in the Nation's Capital: A Review of Academic Options for Students and Parents before the House of Representatives in the District of Columbia.* Statement before the House of Representatives Committee on Government Reform.

Destro, Robert A. June 28, 2002. *Legal Summary of US Supreme Court decision in Zelman v. Simmons-Harris,* 436 US 2002. Retrieved from http://www.edreform.com/school/supreme-court_ruling.html

District of Columbia. 2006. "State Education Office: Summary of Changes." Washington DC: District of Columbia. Government, Retrieved February 12, 2006 from www.dc.gov/seo

District of Columbia Financial Responsibility and Management Assistance Authority. November 12, 1996. *Children in Crisis: The Failure of Public Education in the District.* Retrieved from http://media. washingtonpost.com/wp-srv/local/longterm/library/dc/control/ part1.html

Dobbs, Michael. December 15, 2004. "Charter vs. Traditional: Two Types of DC Public Schools are not Easy to Compare." Retrieved from www.washingtonpost.com

Fagan, T.W. July 2005. *Title I Funds-Who's Gaining and Who's Losing School Year 2005-2006 Update*. Center on Education Policy.

Fain, Paul. 2005. "District of Columbia." *Chronicle of Higher Education.* Vol. 52, No. 1; pp.46-48.

Fitzimmons, J. 2002. "Maine College President wants to Revamp System." *Community College Week*, Vol. 14, Issue 21.

Fixler, D. December 1993. Anatomy of Price Change-The Consumer Price Index: Underlying Concepts and Caveats. *Monthly Labor Review.*

Franzese, L and Osueke, C. 2004. DC Public Schools. *Center for Social Justice.*

Freudenberg, Stacie. 2006. "States Omit Minorities School Scores." *USA Today.*

Friel, Brian. January 2005. "Public or Private School? It's Your Choice." *National Journal.* Vol.37, Issue 1, No. 2, pp. 33-35.

George Washington University. 2006. "More Facts." Washington DC: George Washington University, Retrieved February 10, 2006 from www.gwu.edu

Georgetown University. 2006. "Office of Communication fact Sheets." Washington DC: Georgetown University, Retrieved February 10, 2006 from www.georgetown.edu

Gewertz, Catherine. 2000. "Compromise Plan for DC Governance Stalls." *Education Weekly.* Vol. 19, No. 20; pp. 3-5.

Gibson, James. 2000. "Community and Governance in the Washington DC Schools." *National Civic Review*. Vol. 89, No. 1, pp. 47-51.

Gleason, S. January 23, 1999. "How the NEA Thwarts Education Reform." Paper presented at the 1999 Economic Freedom Forum of CNP. Retrieved from http://www.nrtw.org/b/SHGcnp.html

Goldstein, Amy. June 2006. "Mandate Aside, Private Tutors aren't Always an Option." *The Washington Post.*

Green, R.L. and Griffore, R.J. 1980. "Critical Issues in testing and Achievement of Black Americans: The Impact of Standardized testing on Minority Students." *The Journal of Negro Education*. Vol. 49, No. 3; pp. 238-252.

Greenhouse, S. February 24, 2006. "School Locals Will Let Locals Join Federation." *The New York Times*. Retrieved from http://www.researchnavigator.com/articles/article.asp

Greifner, Laura. "For DC Charter School, Royal Visit Caps Big Year." *Education Week*. Vol. 25, Issue 11.

Hackney Gray, LaRuth. 2004. "The 2004 Charles H. Thompson Lecture-Colloquium Presentation: No Child Left Behind: Opportunities and Threats." *The Journal of Negro Education*. Vol. 74, No. 2; pp. 95-111.

Hamilton, Marci. July 1, 2002. "Why the Supreme Court's Recent Vouchers Opinion was Wrong and also Typical of the Court's Establishment Clause Approach." *FindLaw*. Retrieved from http://writ.findlaw.com/hamilton/20020701.html

Haynes, V. Dion. August 23, 2005. "A Third of DC Principals are New." *The Washington Post*. Retrieved from http://www.washingtonpost.com

Haynes, V. Dion. August 25, 2005. "Charter Schools Expand in Several New Directions." *The Washington Post.*

Haynes, V. Dion. November 22, 2005. "DC School Abandons Charter Bid for Chance at Autonomy." *The Washington Post.*

Haynes, V. Dion. April 22, 2006. "DC Public School Seeks Linkup with New Charter." *The Washington Post.*

Haynes, V. Dion and Lori Montgomery. August 24, 2005. "Report Fans Flames in DC School Funding Debate." *The Washington Post.* Retrieved from http://www.washingtonpost.com

Hendrie, Caroline. October 27, 2004. "Mayors Turn to Charter Schools." *Education Week.* Vol. 24, Issue 9.

Hendrie, Caroline. October 12, 2005. "Capital Charters." *Education Week.* Vol. 25, Issue 7.

Hickock, Eugene. May 9, 2003. *In Search of Education Excellence in the Nation's Capital: A Review of Academic Options for Students and Parents in the District of Columbia.* Statement before the House of Representatives Committee on Government Reform.

Holmes, Eula. 2004. US Congress Approves School Voucher Plan for Nation's Capital. *World Socialist Organization.* Article 27, February 27, 2004.

Honawar, Vaishali. November 2004. "Parental Choice." *Education Week.* Vol. 24, Issue 13; p. 25.

Howard University. 2006. "Howard University Facts." Washington DC: Howard University, Retrieved February 10, 2006 from www. howard.edu

Hsu, Spencer and Justin Blum. 2004. DC Schools Can't Spend US Funds: Senator says System Lacks Adequate Plan for $13 Million. *Washington Post,* Thursday May 20, 2004; pp. B01.

Hurlbut, Richard. 1981. "A Look Back in Time: District of Columbia Public Schools, A Brief History." Retrieved from the World Wide Web: http://www.wikipedia.com

Janey, Clifford B. May 2005. "Declaration of Education: Keeping our Promise to the District's Children." *Strategic Plan.*

Kafer, Krista. 2004. "No Child Left Behind: Where do We go From Here?" The Heritage Foundation. Retrieved October 3, 2005 from http://www.heritage.org

Kafer, Krista and Jonathon Butcher. 2003. How Members of Congress Practice School Choice. *Heritage Foundation Backgrounder*, No. 1684, September 3, 2003.

Kennedy, Sheila S. February 2001. "Privatization Education: The Politics of Vouchers." *Phi Delta Kappan International.* Vol. 82, No. 6.

Kershaw, S. 2000. Schools Turning from Teaching the Trades. *New York Times*, Vol. 149, Issue 51426; pp. A1.

Ladd, Helen. May 9, 2003. *In Search of Education Excellence in the Nation's Capital: A Review of Academic Options for Students and Parents in the District of Columbia.* Statement before the House of Representatives Committee on Government Reform

Ladner, Joyce. March 9, 2003. *Lessons Learned in DC Public Schools: Progress Continues, but Still a Long Way to Go.* Statement before the United States Senate Subcommittee on Oversight of Government Management, Restructuring and the District of Columbia, Committee on Government Affairs.

Lartigue, Casey. November 24, 2002. "When the Mission is Mediocrity: If the DC Public Schools Want to Improve, They'll Need to Aim Higher." *The Cato Institute.* Retrieved from http://www.cato.org

Lartigue, Casey. December 10, 2002. "The Need for Educational Freedom in the Nation's Capital." *The Cato Institute, Policy Analysis*, No. 461.

Lartigue, Casey. May 9, 2003. *In Search of Education Excellence in the Nation's Capital: A Review of Academic Options for Students and Parents in the District of Columbia.* Statement before the House of Representatives Committee on Government Reform.

Lartigue, Casey. October 22, 2003. "Giving DC Kids the Best Education Available." The Cato Institute. Retrieved from http://www.cato.org

Lawrence, L. 1997. Vocational Schooling Mixes with the Mainstream. *Christian Science Monitor*, Vol. 89, Issue 6.

Levessque, K, D. Lauen, P. Teitelbaum, M. Alt, S. Librera and MPR Associates, Inc. 2000. "Vocational Education in the United States: Toward the year 2000." *National Center for Education Statistics*, US Department of Education Research and Improvement; Washington, DC.

Lewis, AC. 2005. Direct from Washington. *Tech Directions*, Vol. 65, Issue 2; pp. 6-7.

Lewis, Laurie, Kyle Snow, Elizabeth Farris, Becky Smerdon, Stephanie Cronen and Jessica Kaplan. 2000. "Condition of America's Public School Facilities: 1999." *NCES 2000 032*. US Department of Education, National Center for Education Statistics.

Lieberman, M. September 5, 2002. *Rolling Back the Teacher Union Juggernaut.*   Retrieved   from   http://www.cato.org/pub_display.php?pub_id=3587&print=y

Long, James E and Eugenia F. Toma. May 1998. "The Determinants of Private School Attendance, 1970-1980." *The Review of Economics and Statistics.* Vol. 70, No.2; pp. 351-357.

Lukas, Carrie. 2003. Moms for School Choice: This One is Really for the Children. *National Review Online*, November 20, 2003. Retrieved from the World Wide Web: http://www.nationalreview.com

Lynette, H. 2000. State Plans Tougher Vocational Curriculum. *New York Times*, Vol. 149, Issue 51413; pp. B5.

Maquire, Steven. July 25, 2001. "Funding School Renovation: Qualified Zone Academy Bonds vs. Traditional Tax-Exempt Bonds." *CRS Report for Congress*. The Library of Congress, Congressional Research Service: Washington, DC.

Marshall, J. Fall 2005. "The Mythology of Teacher Unions." *The Journal of James Madison Institute*. Retrieved from http://www.heartland.org

Matthews, Jay. Tuesday, November 11, 2003. "No child Left Behind Act: Fact and Fiction." *Washington Post*.

McCluskey, N. March 1, 2006. "Controversy Heats Up Over NEA Spending Donations." *The Heartland Institute*.

McElroy, Edward. 2005. "NCLB's Unintended Consequences." *American Teacher*, May.

McGray, D. January 16, 2005. "Working with the Enemy." *The New York Times*.

Mead, Sara. October 2005. "Capital Campaign-Early Returns on District of Columbia Charter Schools." Progressive Policy Institute. Retrieved from http://www.ppionline.org

Mead, Sara. January 22, 2006. "Checklist for Charter Schools." *The Washington Post*.

Mickelson, Heidi H. January 1998. "Trends in the US and an Inside Look at Chicago's Plans." North Central Regional Educational Laboratory. Retrieved from http://ncrel.org/sdrs/pbriefs/97/97-1acct.html

Moore, Nicole. 2005. State Legislators Offer Formula for Improving No Child Left Behind Act. *National Conference of State Legislatures.*

Murdock, DeRoy. 2003. Official Discovery: DC Public Education is a Disaster. *National Review Online,* March 12, 2003. Retrieved March 14, 2006 from the World Wide Web: http://www.nationalreviewonline.com/murdock/murdock031203.asp

Myers, Samuel L. Winter 2004. "The Effect of School Poverty on Racial Gaps in Test Scores: The Case of the Minnesota Basic Standards Test." *Journal of Negro Education.*

NAIS. Fall 2002. "NAIS Board Endorses The Public Purpose of Private Education." *Independent School.* Vol. 62, Issue 1; pp. 3-4.

NAIS. Spring 2004. "How Valuable is an Independent Education?" *Independent School.* Vol. 63, Special Section; p. 5.

NARPAC. 2004. Federal Oversight. *National Association to Restore Pride and Restoration in Americas Capital.* Washington DC. April 5, 2001; pp. 1-18.

National Center for Educational Statistics. "The Nations Report Card, State Profiles." Retrieved September 9, 2005 from http://www.nces.ed.gov/nationsreportcard/states/profile.asp

Norton, Eleanor Holmes. May 9, 2003. *In Search of Education Excellence in the Nation's Capital: A Review of Academic Options for Students and Parents in the District of Columbia.* Statement before the House of Representatives Committee on Government Reform.

Norton, Eleanor Holmes. June 24, 2003. *School Choice in the District of Columbia: Opening Doors for Parents and Students.* Statement before the House of Representatives Committee on Government Reform. Retrieved from http://www.dcpswatch/vouchers.html

Pappas, Max. 2004. Washington Post Supports School Choice: Fred Hiatt Writes a Ringing Endorsement of School Vouchers. *Freedom Works Citizens for a Sound Economy*. Washington DC. Article: February 28, 2004.

Pinkerton, E, N. Kober, C. Scott and B. Buell. October 2003. *Implementing the No Child Left Behind Act: A First Look Inside 15 School Districts in 2002-2003*. Center on Education Policy.

Pohlman, Vernon C. May 1956. "Relationship between Ability, Socio-Economic Status and Choice of Secondary School." *Journal of Educational Sociology*. Vol. 29, No. 9; pp. 392-397.

Polite, Vernon C. Spring 1992. "Getting the Job Done Well: African American Students an Catholic Schools. *The Journal of Negro Education: African American and Independent Schools: Status, Attainment and Issues*. Vol. 61, No. 2; pp. 211-222.

Press Releases. 2004. "Davis Applauds Congressional Reauthorization of DC Tuition Assistance Program." *Congressional Quarterly*, December 6, 2005. Retrieved Aril 21, 2006, Available: LEXIS-NEXIS Academic.

Preston, Jr. Emmett D. October 1940. "The Development of Negro Education in the District of Columbia. *The Journal of Negro Education*. Vol. 9, No. 4; pp. 595-603.

Reid, Karla. 2004. "District of Columbia Schools Facing Leadership Dilemma." *Education Weekly*. Vol. 23, No. 29; pp. 8-9.

Roll Call. 2006. "Norton, Davis Call for Tuition Program Extension." *Hill Talk*, March 6, 2006. Retrieved April 21, 2006, Available: LEXIS-NEXIS Academic.

Sanchez, Claudio. 2004. DC Schools to Test Federal School Voucher Plan. *National Public Radio News*, transcript. January 25, 2004. Retrieved March 13, 2006 from the World Wide Web: http://edre-

form.com/index.cfm?fuseAction=documentID=1730&
sectionID=37

Sarnoff, Joshua. April 19, 2004. *Proposed FY2005 Budget for DCPS*. Statement before the DC Council. Retrieved from http://www.
janeyschool.org/aboutjanney/joshsarnoff.org

Schneider, Mark, J. Buckley and S. Kucsova. 2004. "Making the Grade: Comparing DC Charter Schools to Other DC Public Schools." *Occasional Paper*, No. 71. National Center for the Study of Privatization in Education. Teachers College, Columbia University Scobedeter, G. 2000. Installer Training, Certification Programs Picking up Speed. *Twice: This Week in Consumer Electronics*, Vol. 15, Issue 25.

Sivasubramaniam, Malini. 2003. "History of Education: Selected Moments of the 20th Century." Retrieved March 14, 2006 from the World Wide Web: http://fcis.oise.utoronto.ca/~dschugurensky/
assignment1/1998evenstart.html

Slaughter, Diana T and Deborah J. Johnson. Edited 1998. "Visible Now: Blacks in Private Schools. New York, NY: Greenwood Press.

Smith, Nelson. 2006. Implementing NCLB Across an Evolving Educational Landscape. *Lexington Institute.*

State News Service. 2006. "Davis and Norton Introduce Reauthorization of District of Columbia College Access Act." *State News Service*, March 2, 2006. Retrieved April 21, 2006, Available: LEXIS-NEXIS Academic.

State News Service. 2006. "Government Reform Committee Approves Five-year Extension of DC Tuition Assistance Grant Program." *State News Service*, March 9, 2006. Retrieved April 21, 2006, Available: LEXIS-NEXIS Academic.

Steinberg, B. 1996. Lack of Money Forces Vocational Institute to Close. *Community College Week*, Vol. 9, Issue 8.

Stephens, D. Winter 1983-1984. "President Carter, the Congress and NEA: Creating the Department of Education." *Political Science Quarterly*, pp. 641-663.

Stewart, K.J and S.B. Reed. 1999. "Consumer Price Index Research Series Using Current Methods, 1978-1998." *Monthly Labor Review*, CPI Research Series, June.

Thomas B. Fordham Institute. August 2005. "Charter School Funding: Inequity's Next Frontier." Washington DC.

Toyer, Iris. May 9, 2003. *In Search of Education Excellence in the Nation's Capital: A Review of Academic Options for Students and Parents in the District of Columbia.* Statement before the House of Representatives Committee on Government Reform.

United States Government Accountability Office. May 2005. *Charter Schools-Oversight Practices in the District of Columbia.* Report to Congressional Committees, GAO-05-490.

University of the District of Columbia. 2006. "UDC History." Washington DC: University for the District of Columbia. Retrieved February 10, 2006 from www.udc.edu

University of the District of Columbia. 2006. "UDC Admissions," Washington DC: University of the District of Columbia. Retrieved February 10, 2006 from www.udc.edu/academics/admission.html

US Census Bureau. 2004. Guide to Tabular Presentation. Statistical Abstract of the United States: 2004-2005.

US Census Bureau. 2004. Income 2004-Annual Average Consumer Price Index Research Studies Using Current Measures.Retrieved December 1, 2005 from http://www.census.gov/hhes/www/income/income04/cpiurs.html

US Department of Education. 2002. Reading 2000: Report Card. *National Center for Education Statistics.* Institute of Education Sciences: Washington DC.

US Department of Education. 2004. A Time for Choice: Remarks of Secretary Paige at the Heritage Foundation. Released January 8, 2004.

US Department of Education. "Fact Sheet on the Major Provisions of the Conference Report to HR 1, the No Child Left Behind Act." Retrieved September 11, 2005 from http://www.ed. gov/nclb/overview/intro/factsheet.html

US Department of Education. 2006. "Secretary Spelling Delivers Remarks on School Choice. Released April 5, 2006." Retrieved April 28, 2006 from the World Wide Web: http://www.ed. gov/print/news/pressreleases/2006/04/04052006.html

Warren, Donald R. 1974. "The US Department of Education: A Reconstruction Promise to Black Americans." *The Journal of Negro Education* 43, 4: 437-445.

Wells, Amy S. December 29, 2004. "Charter Schools: Lessons in Limits." *The Washington Post.*

Williams, Anthony. May 9, 2003. *In Search of Education Excellence in the Nation's Capital: A Review of Academic Options for Students and Parents in the District of Columbia.* Statement before the House of Representatives Committee on Government Reform.

Wolf, Issac. September 27, 2005. "Success of DC Charts Course for Charter Schools." *Kansas City infoZine.* Retrieved from http:// www.infozine.com/news/stories

Wolf, Patrick, B. Gutmann, N. Eissa, M. Puma and M. Silverberg. April 5, 2005. *Evaluation of the DC Opportunity Scholarship Program: First Year Report of Participation.* US Department of Education, National Center for Education Evaluation and Regional Assistance.

Washington DC: US Government Printing Office.

Wolf, Patrick, William Howell and Paul Peterson. 2000. "School Choice in Washington DC: An Evaluation after One Year." *Conference on Vouchers and Public Education*, March 2000. Cambridge, MA: Harvard University Press.

Wrinkle, Robert D, Joseph Stewart and J.L. Polinard. October 1999. "Public School Quality, Private Schools and Race." *American Journal of Political Science*. Vol. 43, No. 4; pp. 1248-1253.

World Wide Web Sites

www.aisgw.org/about.asp

www.census.gov/hhes/www/income/income04/spiurs.html

www.cew.wise.edu/charterschools/practicesattachments.chavez/chessie_moquete_thesis.pdf

www.dcfordemocracy.org

www.dcgop.com/grassroots_maultsby.html

www.dcpswatch.com/dcps/0401.html

www.k12.dc.us/dcps/home.html

www.leaderu.com/orgs/probe/docs/nea.html

www.modernizations.org/FAQas.html

www.nais.org/about/index.cfm?itemnumber+145842

www.ncspe.org

www.nea.org

www.nea.org/aountnea/mission.html

www.pfaw.org

www.washingtonian.com/schools/private/2004/coedprivate04.html

About the Editor

Abdul Karim Bangura is a professor of Political Science and Research Methodology in the Department of Political Science at Howard University in Washington, DC. He holds a Ph.D. in Political Science, a Ph.D. in Development Economics, a Ph.D. in Linguistics, and a Ph.D. in Computer Science. He is the author and/or editor of 57 other books and more than 400 scholarly articles. He is the recipient of numerous scholarly and community service awards. He is fluent in about a dozen African languages and six European languages, and is now studying to increase his competency in Arabic and Hebrew.

978-0-595-48033-3
0-595-48033-0